BECOMING SANTA

Richard Robbins

Dedicated to my wife, Fara, who truly personifies
the Spirit of Christmas throughout her life

Printed in the United States of America

Second Printing 2013

ISBN 987-0-9829877-4-2

Quill Publishing
82 South 740 East
American Fork, Utah 84003
(801) 597-6923

CHAPTERS

Richard Robbins

1

How I Became a Santa

Folks shouldn't have to worry about lifestyle changes when they've grown older. They should be somewhat settled in and be in a position where they can sit back in familiar and comfortable surroundings and enjoy the benefits of their lifelong labors. There may be a few regrets they have to live with. I've never known anyone who's grown old and not made a few mistakes along the way, but then I've also never known anyone who can't look back with a little pride at noteworthy accomplishments.

One thing for sure is that those approaching retirement tend to mull over their lives and at some point consider if what they've done is what they should have been doing. That is to say, many people have settled for a job because it was convenient, the pay was acceptable, it was in the proper location, and so forth instead of maybe following an aspiration.

I've had friends, relatives, and just acquaintances that, because of a cutback or a company problem, were placed in the position of having to look for different employment. Most of them, just to keep bread on the table, have had to settle for the first job that came along. Sometimes it's a better job than the one they left, after all, they're more experienced. But in most cases, they've taken a cut in pay or a lesser job.

And then there are those fortunate enough to be able to get it right the second time around. Their original job dissatisfaction directed them to follow a dream or do what they had always wanted to do.

Well, as you may have figured out by now, one day I found myself in a quandary about my job and life. I found myself wondering, *Is what I've been doing all my life what I was supposed to do? Or is there a different, perfect purpose for my existence? It might be more than I'm doing now, or it might even be less. But there's probably something for which I am absolutely suited.*

Don't get me wrong. I've always been satisfied with my life's work, and I've done my share of good. But there are always questions. *Should I have done something different? Could my life have been more complete? Did I have more to offer?*

It seems like the older I get, the more I reflect about my life. Maybe it just takes longer to figure out the right answers because there's so much more to remember at my age. In any event, such thoughts have taken on a greater significance to me as age has set in and most of my life is behind me.

An incident that happened in my life led me to this quandary. In retrospect, I wondered how many lives have been redirected for the better—when what was thought of as an adverse event caused a change in the direction taken. The assessment of whether a setback or a blessing has occurred can be determined only after the results of the forced change have been concluded. This incident in my case involved a change in my lifelong employment that took me from being a very successful businessperson to being a Santa Claus in less than a month's time. I wish I could say that I landed in this new vocation after much contemplation and that I planned every move, but it more or less just happened because of a series of events.

I never in my life had an inclination, or even an urge, to play the role of Santa Claus. A need merely appeared and probably had the results it did because of my nature. As I have done throughout my life, once I accepted the fact that a change must be made, or that something must be done, I approached it with enthusiasm. It's not in my nature to be mediocre. At the time, I thought to myself, *If I'm going to be Santa Claus, I'm not going to be just any old run-of-the-mill Santa; I have to be the best Santa ever.*

I reasoned that being the best Santa would fit into my plan because it would secure me more work, which equated to a larger income. And that was what was needed. I merely took on the job of a Santa because at the time I needed extra money. I never felt embarrassment and never felt uncomfortable about playing Santa. I thought, *If it's done properly, it's as dignified as any job. Any work can cause a person to be proud if it's done as it should be.* At the outset, of course, there was no way of knowing how much this new role would impact my life, and I might even say the lives of others.

I knew even before starting that I could be a good Santa. I certainly love children. I've often, while shopping at a grocery store or elsewhere, stopped to look into the face of a beautiful child. I've even sneaked a tweak of a toe or pinched a cheek when I could, and I've spent a lot of my time coaxing a smile out of toddlers. These things, of course, were all done behind the parents' back while they were picking up a bottle of jam or something else. I'm sure they would have thought me a fool if they had seen my antics.

It doesn't matter the age of the child. I've thought it the height of joy to watch an elementary-aged child grasp a new idea. Such children are so full of wonderment and so ready to participate in life. It's fun to be the one responsible for placing even one small but good thought in their minds. Any job that would bring me and children together had to be agreeable. I've always been happy when I've been in the presence of a child.

I'd even gotten along great with teens. They aren't mine, so I can enjoy them. One of their great rites of passage into adulthood is to finally find out that Santa isn't real. This can be a lot of fun if handled right. Teens that are testing the boundaries of life always cause a challenge, but I've found them very reasonable and always wanting a listening ear. To me, teens have never been a challenge; they are an opportunity. I could never blame teenagers for their actions because I believe they are simply what society has made them. If we want better teens, we should be better adults.

And that brings me to the world of adults. For as long as I can remember, my thinking about adults and Santa Claus has been fairly straightforward. Being a Santa for a grownup could be the most enjoyable of all experiences, I would be in a position to get acquainted with many more adults. There's never been an adult who hasn't made me a better person for having known him or her. I never met anyone that didn't know something I didn't know. This ruling class has many little idiosyncrasies that are fun to play with. Adults seem to let their guard down a bit and be more susceptible to having a good time around a Santa. With their guard down, it's easier to be a loving Father Christmas image. Most will take a little ribbing or even advice from a person whom they feel an affinity toward. They have known Santa all their lives and have developed a trusted kinship.

It is certain that Santa should have a good effect on all he meets; he is destined to make the world a better place to live. I've always believed that people don't have to change a lot to be a lot better. I've always believed that adults will improve if they can bring out the child in themselves. The wonders and miracles of Christmas will bring memories of days gone by, most are good memories. Good memories need repeating; reliving them and sharing them with family helps us to re-prioritize life's values.

Being a Santa would be a new experience for me. Its possibility was born out of necessity, but its birth seemed to give me new life.

In three months, I would reach my sixty-fifth birthday. That was the day I had set to retire from my lifelong career, and I was looking forward to spending more time with Sarah, my mate of forty-five years. My job wasn't the kind that I just couldn't wait to get away from. I've never dreaded getting up and going to work. I've loved my work and especially those I've worked with. I've always been treated fairly and for the last thirty-five years had missed only three days of work, even then I stayed home only because I didn't want to give those at work what I had contacted. My work was just challenging enough to stretch my mind but not hard enough to snap it.

I looked at retirement as leaving something that was great and going on to something even better. I never experienced any remorse about retiring from the company because I've always given it all I had to give. When I brought up the subject of my future retirement after I turned 64, those I worked for said they would deeply miss me, "But if anyone can go away with a good conscience, you can." I never thought of slacking off at the end of my employment. I wanted to leave my work in order, to be passed to my successor cleanly and without concern. I was totally devoted because I felt that they, in turn, were loyal to me.

One month earlier, I arose, had my usual breakfast, a Carnation drink and a piece of toast, read the headlines in the newspaper, checked the sports, and left for work. On arriving at work, I was told that Joe wanted to see me in his office. This was a regular occurrence, as Joe was the vice president of marketing. I worked in his department as customer service manager. I was a little surprised at seeing Jordan Green there also when I arrived. Jordan was the president of the company. I took my usual seat and could tell this was going to be a somber occasion.

Joe never got three words out of his mouth before he broke down. Tears came to his eyes, and he had a difficult time going on. I looked to Jordan, and his eyes were watering also.

Joe said, "I'm sorry, Bob, but we don't have good news."

I nodded my head, which gave him strength to go on. He said, "Bob, we're being forced into a bankruptcy; we've taken every possible step we could think of. We've even tried to find a buyer for the company, and we have no alternatives. We've recently lost several large accounts because we are just too small to compete with the national discount chains. We wanted to tell you in person so you wouldn't get this information second hand."

Joe got up, came around the desk to me, threw his arms around me, and just kept saying, "We're sorry!" over and over again. It wasn't long until Jordan joined us. His sorrow was especially sincere; I felt it deep down in my soul.

My first reaction was to feel a real sadness for both of them. I was losing a job; each of them were losing their life's work. I could leave and be done with it; there were many consequences they would have to face. I assured them that they had done all they could; this assurance helped them pull themselves together.

We discussed all the implications. They seemed to be asking for and relying on my input a great deal. I believe these two men who had never done a bad thing in their lives or had never made a bad business decision were being penalized by changing times. They needed to know they are still admired and, yes, even loved. I assured them that a failure of a business isn't a personal failure unless you have failed to do what you thought was right. They had never neglected any facet of their business, and they had never underestimated the competition. They just didn't have the equal funding to keep up with their competitors.

I was informed that the bankruptcy would be immediate so they could stop further bleeding and that all company funds were already tied up. Of course this meant my retirement funds as well. It was a very unpleasant thought that all I had planned for was suddenly diminished to zilch. Most often, a man who has just lost his job will ask himself how he will ever be able to go home and tell his wife. This was the least of my worries. My wife has always supported me and has believed that I would always make things right. The best thing about her was that she was never demanding; she was thankful for what she had and grateful for any added blessings, as she called them.

I was told I could gather up my things and shouldn't worry about coming back; there was simply no work left to do. I gathered those items that were personally mine. After letting Joe and Jordan know that I was only a telephone call away if needed and saying goodbye to my colleagues I left to go home.

The drive home didn't seem much different than those of any other day except for the fact that there was less traffic because of the earlier hour. I didn't seem to fall apart; after all, I had been provided a good life. True, I hadn't amassed a fortune because I had put a couple of kids through school and because other incidents had drained the budget occasionally. We had enough to live for a while. I never worried through the years of my employment because my retirement had been well planned for through a company plan.

Of course, there are those who might think me stupid for putting all my eggs in one basket, but in retrospect, I would probably do it all over again. A decision can be judged only by its outcome; it doesn't mean that the decision was not the right one to be made at the time. I reconciled myself with the belief that no matter where I had put my funds, because of some other adverse events that were very prevalent in society today, I might find myself in the same boat. Whatever line of thought I pursued, I never really felt bad. The only thing that had changed was my financial situation. I was still the same man.

When I arrived home, I was to the point of really feeling okay. Sarah met me at the door and said, "You're home early."

I put my arms around her and said, "Honey, I'm home forever."

As always, she assumed the best and said, "Oh my! Did they let you retire early?"

I said, "The whole company is retiring."

Not wanting to drag out the suspense or cause her any undo alarm, I got right to the point. After I rehearsed all that had happened, her only response was, "Oh, those poor boys, will they be all right Robert?"

I told her it would be hard on them but they were strong and would pull through it all right. I asked her if she was all right or had any worries. She merely said, "I never worry because I have you." And then she added, "We'll make do; we always do."

Her "make-do" philosophy had guided me through our forty-five years of marriage. All that was important was making do; we didn't need a lot of extras to enjoy life. She then added, "Things usually always happen for the best."

I never imagined then how right she was.

For the next few days, we considered all our alternatives. We evaluated our needs to determine if we had enough resources to meet them. Thankfully, we had saved some money to get us by for a while, but in the end, we determined that I would definitely have to find another source of income somewhere. Our house was paid off, and I had already planned to start my

Social Security at 65. We certainly weren't going to starve. Some company somewhere was certainly in need of a seasoned public relations person. I wasn't in a hurry; it was kind of nice having some time for working on a few ignored household chores.

After a week of putting it off, I took steps to see what the job market had to offer. After all these years, it felt funny imagining the task of setting up my own job interviews. I knew all the ins and outs of interviewing because I had interviewed and hired hundreds of prospects for company positions over the last 35 years. I drew up a very impressive resume and said to myself after I looked it over, *I'd hire that guy!*

Choosing four or five companies that were advertising for people with my skills, I sent resumes to them and waited for them to start competing for my services. In the meantime, I called a few companies we had done business with to see if they had any openings. The answers seemed quite standard: "Not at the time. We'll put your name in our file, though. Good luck!" The calls always ended with, "You're a good man, and you should find a job easily."

When my resumes hadn't turned up a single result, I decided to call the companies I had sent them to. I wanted to see if they had filled the position yet or if they were considering my resume. I made contact with one young executive who said, "I wish you were younger. You sound like just what we're looking for, but, to be honest, Mr. Field, in the past have *you* ever hired someone who was within a few months of retirement age?"

Yes, he was a smart young man. He told me I was too old without having to say it. I tweaked my resume to imply that I was young for my age and sent several more inquiries out, but I ended up with the same results. I told my wife I was too old to get employment, and she said, "They just haven't seen how young you look."

With that advice, I found a couple more promising companies and decided to go in person to show them I was not an old
man. At one stop, a secretary who had obviously been given the
authority to pre-screen applicants told me to fill out an employment application form. The form was inclusive and took most of
the afternoon just to complete. I took the form and my resume
to the secretary and was told they would be in touch with me. I
thought to myself, *That's the last time I'll hear from them. Why do
they say it and never do it?* I felt like saying, "When you call, just
ask for Mr. Blue because that's the color I'll be from holding my
breath while waiting to hear from you."

I actually had an interview at the second company I visited
that day. I'll ever be grateful to a young woman executive who
had a father my age and who took compassion on me. She said,
"Mr. Field, I read your resume and was more than impressed. I
would first like to say how sorry I am to hear about your company's termination. I would love to have an employee just like you
who would stay with us that long and prove to be such an asset.
The problem is that that is exactly what we're looking for—
someone who can be with us for a long time. It's very evident
that you have some good years left in you, but we can't afford to
hire, train, and then have to hire again soon and go through the
time and expense of training all over again."

Then she asked the clincher question, "Do you see what I
mean?"

What could an honest person's answer be? I assured her that
I understood, that she was right, and that I appreciated her for
being straight with me. I left but knew from that moment on,
even in my own mind, that I couldn't be an asset to any company
at my age. It probably wasn't even fair of me to ask someone to
take me on. I determined to stop the process I was following.

I went home and told Sarah my dilemma. She said, "Well,
don't worry; something will come up."

That night after Sarah retired; I grabbed a pad and pencil and started thinking. I always think better with a pad and pencil in hand. I wrote, *What would I really like to do at my age?* I had done this when I was young and was considering what my life's work would be. The first thing I put on my list back when I was young and what I started my new list with now was, *I like to work with people.* I had made the right decision back then and, as a result, had experienced a very enjoyable career. I had been told on several occasions that I had an innate instinct as to people's needs and a natural way of understanding human behavior. As I looked back, I remembered that I had been thanked more than once for setting people in the right direction or helping them realize their potential and how to reach it. To me, this was very rewarding work.

These reflections led me to ask myself what the second thing on the list way back then was. I couldn't answer exactly, but I know it was something like, *What career would allow this to happen?* I think that back then I listed several occupations that would permit me to be involved with people. And then, on my new list, I ended each of the two items with *at my age.* I knew if I thought hard enough and did my research diligently, I could come up with a proper solution.

Just before placing the pad down and determining to give it more thought in the morning, I had a thought come to my mind, and I decided to scribble a note as a reminder to give my thought some attention later. I reflected that Christmas was only two and a half months away. My wife loved Christmas and went all out every year with the many traditions we had built over a lifetime. I couldn't let her down by not providing for the season she so loved. I knew I needed to get more funds in the next two and a half months. Beneath the two items on my list, I jotted down one word, *Christmas,* just as a reminder. I left the pad and pencil on the table and went to bed.

The next morning, as usual, Sarah arose before I did. She always straightens up the house the first thing every morning. She picked up the pad I had left on the table and read the list:

1. I like to work with people. How can I do this at my age?

2. What career would allow this to happen at my age?

Christmas

She saw that it was a work in progress, so she put the pad down and placed the pencil back on the table. She then picked up the pencil again and put the number three in front of Christmas, assuming it was a list item. I came down about half an hour later; Sarah was dusting and singing about the house and seemed to be in a happy mood.

I asked, "What makes you so happy this morning?"

She said, "Oh, Robert, I knew you would come up with a great idea."

I was a little confused, and then she said, "I read your notes on the pad. I know you like people, so what better career than a Christmas job? It's the best time of the year for people because they're always so much happier. What do you plan to do?"

I took a quick look at the pad and saw the number "3" written in just before my reminder note, *Christmas*.

I thought I would play along with her misunderstanding, so I said, "Well, Walmart always needs more help at that time of the year, so I thought I would apply for a job as a door greeter."

She didn't lose any of her enthusiasm as she said, "You would make a marvelous greeter; they are all so nice and help in so many ways. Can you imagine with your experience how much they would all love you?"

Then she showed some concern in her facial expressions and said, "But you'd have to be on your feet all day, and that would be so hard at your age."

I decided to take it one step further. "Well maybe I could be a Santa Claus. They get to sit a lot, and it doesn't seem to me to be very hard work."

She picked this idea up as though it were pure inspiration. She had the whole concept in her head before I could even tell her why I wrote *Christmas* on the list. She said, "I'll get started on a Santa outfit right away. I've always wanted to dress Santa in a proper suit. Look at you; you look like the real Santa. Your face is so kind, and I've been meaning to tell you that your belly is getting a little round. Now you go do your business thing and find out the best place for Santa to work. I have to get busy here because I have plenty to do."

I have always loved Sarah for her commitment to a job. Her enthusiasm was catching, and I found myself laughing at the thought at first but then thinking, *Why not? It'll at least get us through Christmas, and I can then concentrate on what to do next.*

The more I thought about it, the more it became a possibility. Besides, she was a wonderful seamstress, and I couldn't wait to see the great outfit she had in mind. After taking a full appraisal of my jolly belly, I decided to do Santa research the rest of the day. A feasibility study would tell me if I needed to put the brakes on this idea.

2

Preparing For Business

To my surprise, I found from my research that being a Santa could be quite lucrative. Its only setback is that it's seasonal work. I discovered I could work at a mall all day for a wage that was far above average. Further, large corporate parties always needed a good Santa, and I could work several parties a night. Even private parties offered good possibilities. I got to thinking how much fun it would be to drop in at a hospital or an elderly folk's center. *No money for Santa at those places,* I muttered to myself. But then I backtracked and thought, *There are many different forms of payment, some of which are much better than money.*

My first hurdle came when I tried to treat being Santa as a business project. I thought I might be taking the real meaning out of Christmas if I treated my prospective role as a Santa Claus as just another business. After all, Santa himself was never in it for the money; all he wanted to do was share happiness and love.

At lunch that day, without having thought much more about it, I mentioned this problem to Sarah. She said, "How could Santa make all those toys and get around visiting all the boys and girls if he didn't plan for some way to do it? And Robert, if Santa didn't eat, he wouldn't have the strength to get everything done he has to do. He has to get money from somewhere. I'm sure he has to have a house and even a factory up at the North Pole. If he didn't run this all properly, he would really have a mess with everything he has to do. I think you could call that some kind of a business, couldn't you?"

I was reconciled and even felt good about my new "business venture." It would fit right in; I definitely knew how to run a business.

My next problem was time. Here it was almost the last of September with the main Christmas push starting right after Thanksgiving. If I was going to secure a Santa position in a mall, I had to get moving. *I might already be too late*, I thought to myself. We had three major malls in our city, any one of which would serve my purposes. I would need to visit each mall and apply for the job almost immediately.

This brought me to the next problem, which I verbalized to myself. *No one is going to hire me if they can't see me in my Santa suit. Priority one—I have to get my Santa uniform.*

I hated calling it a uniform, Santa surely doesn't get up in the morning and say to his elves, "Bring me my uniform." To him it's not an outfit he's required to wear as a symbol of his work. It's the clothing he loves because it's cheery and keeps him warm.

I went to Sarah and asked how long she thought it might take to finish my Santa clothes. That sounded kind of good: "Santa Claus clothes."

She started making a vocal list: "Pick up the fabric, the braiding, the gold thread; find real white fur; find just the right belt and boots; sewing time; stitching time." She stopped abruptly and said, "When do you need it?"

I laid out my dilemma to her and she just stated, "Oh my, I'll have to get started right away." And then she mumbled to herself as she walked off, "Maybe I could get Mabel to help and even Ann; Ann is such a great seamstress."

Although I never got my answer I knew everything possible would be done to hurry up production. I went in the kitchen ten minutes later and heard Sarah on the phone. I could tell it was Ann she was talking to. Sarah said, "Mabel said she could come over in a half hour. Would that be all right with you?"

A half hour later, the doorbell rang. Ann and Mabel arrived at the same time. They were all business and just gave me a nod. I stayed out of the way as always when these three were in cahoots, but curiosity did get the best of me. I stood outside the kitchen door to hear what was going on.

Sarah was the first to speak. She said, "I'm going to sew a Santa outfit for Robert, and I want it to be the best set of clothes Santa has ever worn. I need to do it in a hurry, and that's why I've called you here to ask for your help."

It was very evident from Ann's and Mabel's reactions that they had just been handed the holy grail of sewing. They couldn't wait to get started. According to their thinking, the best fabric shop was forty miles away in the next city. They would leave in an hour and gather the finest material and supplies offered on the market. While there, Anne said she knew of a leather shop that did custom work. They would check that out for the perfect belt. And Mable said, "Oh, a robe! He must have a beautiful robe."

My first thought was, *Well this idea has **already** brought happiness to three women.*

I laughed to myself as I thought of the Santa's workshop I would have in my house tomorrow. I even laughed more when I thought, *Well, I have my first elves—Mabel and Ann.*

Mabel was almost eighty years old, but she was one of those perpetual-motion people. If there wasn't a job to do, she would invent one. We often laughed that she must run on Energizer batteries. Sarah always raved over the beautiful array of fine clothes Mabel had sewn, including a baptismal dress for a granddaughter and a prom formal for another granddaughter. She had once even reupholstered a sofa for her sun-room, and it was the pride of her house.

Ann was "Mrs. Steady," a veritable encyclopedia of facts. She knew where to get everything and at the best price and she always seemed to be available when needed.

I had grown to love these two ladies. Their personalities made them shine; and yes, I often called them beautiful, which always brought the response, "Oh you . . ." with an added giggle.

With that crew, I knew it wouldn't take long to have a fine outfit; so with that obstacle behind me, I went ahead with my other plans. I thought, *I have to make a list.* And then I laughed as I thought and even sang a little, "Checking it twice!" I found out later that Santa makes a lot of lists. I had to list everything that needed to be done to get me out there on my first job.

I didn't like the word "job," so I spent a minute thinking about what I should call my appointments. *Let's see, 'job,' 'work,' 'trade,' 'occupation,' 'profession,' or 'post'?* None sounded acceptable. *How about calling it my 'task' or 'duty' or even 'mission'?* I asked myself. *That's not bad; why not call each undertaking a 'mission'?*

I settled on that for the time being. I could hear Sarah asking, "What's your mission tonight, Santa?" I thought if I named it "my mission," it would sound more like a self-imposed assignment to be accomplished rather than something I was compelled to do every day. I laughed at myself again as I thought, *Why not just take the 's' off 'self' and it would be an 'elf-appointed assignment'?* I was just having a little fun.

I also, right then, determined that each Santa visit had to have an objective. All missions have objectives. All of these fun thoughts were swept aside when it simply came to me. All of Santa's appointments are called "visits." I had just learned my first lesson about being Santa, don't try to change anything about him, he has been pretty successful for several centuries doing the same thing over and over. So I made a things-to-do list, which went something like this:

1. Determine clientele

2. Appraise competition

3. Do a cost analysis

4. Draw up marketing plan

5. Design marketing material, letterhead, envelopes, business cards, promotional flyers, etc.

6. Set up a Post Office box to receive mail anonymously

7. Get an appointment calendar

8. Memorize all reindeer names

9. Go over Christmas carols and songs

10. Set up credit-card procedures

11. Practice my ho, ho, ho routine

12. Grow a beard

13. Work on a good Santa program

14. Get a good Santa promotional picture

Then I wrote myself a note: *Never do anything in any way that will bring discredit to Santa Claus.* I was moved to make this note after the last item on the list. After all, Santa and I were going to be the same person. The list was enough to keep me busy for a while, but I was sure other items would present themselves as needed.

I had always loved a challenge and seemed to have one here. This work was fun. I started staying up longer and getting up earlier just to get things done. I started wondering if this is how the real Santa feels. I thought to myself, *Can you imagine how satisfying each workday must be for him?*

I was beginning to think there is a real Santa. I believe that most people think that Santa isn't real, but I think that all people wished he were. *Wishes and hopes are what keep us motivated in life*, I reminded myself. Hope is more than a dream, it is a way of making a dream become a reality. Hope is the feeling that the bad feeling you are experiencing won't be permanent.

I determined that I would ask one question before any business decisions were finalized in the future. This question eventually became the "company" motto, and I had to ask it many more times than I thought I would. The question was, *What would Santa do in this situation?* Once the answer to this question was evaluated, the solution would become policy.

On a whim, I called Barb Barwick. She had worked as the design director in our marketing department, and we had worked well together.

She answered on the first ring. I said, "Barb, its Robert Field. Have you found any work yet?"

She said that she was still looking but had several good prospects, and then she asked me what I was up to. When I told her my plan to be Santa, she was amazed. She told me that just before everything fell apart at work, she had suggested that they use me this year as the company Santa. "You'll make a great Santa," she said.

I had often thought that Barb had good powers of observation, and I enjoyed the confidence builder. I told her I was calling because I needed some letterhead, business cards, and envelopes designed. I told her I wouldn't be able to pay her a lot. She stopped me right there and said, "Robert, you'll pay me nothing. It's not that I don't have time on my hands with nothing to do. It'll be a fun diversion and will allow me to repay you for all the times you've helped me."

She then said what I loved to hear, "Robert, it will be a labor of love, and you'll have the best Santa material available." She gave out a little giggle and said, "I'll be Santa's little helper."

I thought to myself, *Elf number three.*

I gave her the necessary information, told her to leave the address blank, and pointed out that I would call her back with a Post Office box number. I wanted only a Post Office box number and a cell phone number on the card. I don't know why, but I really didn't want people to know who I was or where I lived. Thinking out loud, I said, *I must be able to do something so that people don't have all that information about me. Santa and I have one thing in common—anonymity. We both like our privacy and like to stay in the background.*

Then an idea came to me, *Why not? Why do I have to put my real name on the card at all? Why not just Santa Claus? That's all they really have to know me by, and that's what I want to be known by.*

I didn't want anyone saying upon my arrival, "We're pleased to have you come over, Robert." That would take me right out of character. But, if they called me "Santa," they and I would truly think of me as Santa.

Over the next few days, I worked on my list. I made arrangements for a Post Office box, got a private cell phone and number, recorded a perfect answering message, sent this information over to Barb via email, memorized the reindeer' names with the help of the song, "Rudolph the Red-Nosed Reindeer," contracted with a credit-card acceptance company, and then spent most of my time working on my marketing plan.

It turned out that I had a much larger potential clientele than I had envisioned. Besides the three major malls, there were over twelve hundred companies, an Associated Stores group that represented most of the downtown stores, and strip malls in the area. I listed some of the departments of government that might have Christmas parties and was surprised at how many there were. From there, I started collecting names, addresses, and phone numbers of those in charge of Christmas parties. My plan was to contact each person to inform her or him of my credentials and the nature of my visits. I would leave everybody several promotional flyers and a good number of business cards. I would always ask for references and the names of those they knew who might have the need for a good Santa. After prioritizing the companies to determine where my major effort should be directed, I still had a list of about four hundred possible clients.

It was time to sit down and draw up my promotional flyer. In the past, I had helped with a few marketing campaigns and had come up with pretty good ideas for promoting some of our products. I had full faith in my abilities and knew I could do as well as anyone. But after an hour of thinking, I was drawing blanks. Sarah brought me some milk and cookies she had just baked and asked how it was going. I told her I wanted to say just the right thing in the flyer but was having a hard time coming up with it. She said, "What is it that you want to tell them?"

I said, "That I need work, that I'm good, hire me."

She instructed me that Santa never needed work—there was always more than he could get done. He just needed to make sure he could fit everything in properly. She left the room; I ate a cookie, had a sip of milk, and sat back and wrote:

Hi!
It's Santa again, another year, boy they come by fast, ho, ho, ho.
This is the time of year that I get very busy. Don't worry, I definitely want to come to your Christmas party and will make the time to be there.

Will you please just let me know when it is and what would be a good time to arrive?

Just call me and we will discuss my visit.
Phone number at the North Pole:
842-667-7653

The-Nor-Pole

P.S. I usually charge less than it would cost to rent a Santa costume.

Of course this had to be printed on beautiful card stock with just the right color of dark-red printing ink. And it had to be delivered in an envelope with the words handwritten on the outside, *From Santa*, and under that *Merry Christmas*.

I thought it important to size up my competition. As far as I could gather from listings and the Chamber of Commerce, there were only three other professional Santa's in the area. And from what I could learn, none of them was very proficient or skilled at his work. Besides, there was a lot more work than three Santa's could handle. The largest competition would come from those who chose to have a Santa from within their own company. They usually had very shabby, rented costumes that didn't fit very well. They were most often men of standing in their companies, and they had no particular talent for being Santa. Most of them didn't want to be Santa in the first place and did it only after a little coercion. The bottom line was that I was needed; competition virtually did not exist. Another motto entered my mind, *Everyone deserves a good Santa.*

3

My Santa Suit

I started growing a beard the minute I decided to be Santa. I had started going prematurely gray in my late forties, and my hair was now, as Sarah called it, "A beautiful white." I didn't like white hair then but thought it most convenient now.

I never had grown a beard in my life and didn't even know what I'd look like with one. I hoped it would be the same color as my hair. I knew I would have to let my hair grow out a little also.

I've never liked Santa's with long, straggly beards; to me, these Santa's always seem to be a little intimidating and sometimes even scary to a young person. And no matter what they did with their beards, neither the Santa's nor the beards look believable. No, a nice, neatly trimmed, mid-sized beard is what I imagined for me. And I determined that definitely I could not tolerate a fake beard. I have seen fake beards discolored around the mouth from constant wear, and every Santa wearing one looks downright uncomfortable, they were always having to adjust the beard and seemed to be forever pulling hair out of their mouths. I said to Sarah, "I want a beard that can be *pulled*. I certainly don't want to be concerned with a beard when I should be concerned with a child."

I practiced saying "Ho, ho, ho" very seriously, as that's the thing children hear first and the thing they hear most often from a Santa. A good "Ho, ho, ho" should set the stage for a visit from Santa. I've heard Santa's who believed they had to use a very low, guttural sound with their voices, but to me, such laughter never sounds like a really jolly laugh should sound. I observed a Santa at one time who sounded almost evil, and I found myself wishing he would stop.

In my opinion, nearly every "Ho, ho, ho" I've heard from Santa's sounds meaningless and without conviction. After trying a few of them, I could see what I was up against because no matter what I did, they just didn't sound right. I went back to my motto, *What would Santa do in this situation?* It was quite a revelation when I thought to myself, *Santa really loves all people, and when he sees them together to celebrate his favorite holiday, it pleases him to no end. When he comes out and receives their applause and hears them singing any number of Santa songs, it right out tickles him, and he just has to laugh. It doesn't matter about the pitch or the rumbling depth. All that matters is the real happiness of the moment, and the laugh has to come right from his jolly, round belly. I can do that.*

So the first thing I did was stop practicing saying "Ho, ho, ho" because I wanted it to just come out naturally. I got so I loved to laugh and seemed to be doing it more often. The result wasn't quite right yet, but I knew it would come.

It's one thing to sell oneself as a great Santa—to have everything in line, including a great outfit, beard, and so forth. But it's another thing to *be* a great Santa. If Santa doesn't deliver at the actual visit, it's all for naught. As a future Santa, I knew I was going to become an entertainer—more than that, a professional entertainer. I said to myself, *I don't have to just act the role of Santa Claus; I have to actually* be *Santa.*

Santa has the largest fan club in the world and cannot let his fans down. I can dance and sing and have done so on several occasions, but I didn't think this was the kind of entertaining Santa believers were looking for. *They go to the mall or a party just for the Christmas spirit*, I thought. *And if they arrive without it, I have to make sure they get it. How would Santa pull that off?*

I knew that the words "Merry Christmas" had to be included. A lot of folks have started using the term "Happy Christmas" or have left out the "Christmas" and replaced it with "holidays." They never give Christmas its individual respect but just group it in with New Year's. "Happy Christmas" doesn't sound like the real thing to me. It's like saying, "Have a delightful or pleasing or contented Christmas." I want people to have a joyful, cheerful, smiley, jolly, uplifting Christmas. "Merry" seems to contribute to the spirit; "happy" is just sitting back and acknowledging its presence. And "Happy New Year's" has enough emphasis to stand on its own.

I started gathering up Santa material—jokes, stories, sayings, or anything that would allow me to make people happy. I wrote scripts for each occasion—company parties, children visits, even visits to hospitals and homes for the elderly. It was fun. Good material was out there, and I had a good time fitting it to my personality. I practiced what I would say, how I would say it, and what my objective would be on each visit. Thank goodness most of my visits would be rather short. The downside was that I wasn't going to have a lot of time to promote Santa and the spirit of Christmas, so I had to be very efficient with the time I had.

About two weeks to the day I had decided to be a Santa, Sarah came into my office and said, "Do we have anything on tomorrow night?"

I told her that nothing was scheduled, and she in turn told me to "keep it free" from about 7:00PM on. When I asked her what we were going to do, she said, "Just keep it free."

The phone rang, and it was Barb Barwick. She said she had the material completed and was going to be in the neighborhood about 7:00PM tomorrow night and wanted to know if she could drop it off. After I told her to hold on for a minute, I told Sarah what was going on. She said, "That would be lovely; tell her to definitely stop by."

After telling Barb that tomorrow evening would be great, I hung up the phone and said to Sarah, "I thought we were supposed to keep the night free." She just smiled, turned around, and walked out.

That's when I discovered that curiosity not only might kill the cat but also can do damage to Santa. I wasn't too functional the rest of the night. And most of the next day was almost like waiting for Christmas.

Well, 7:00PM arrived the next night, and right on time the doorbell rang. I thought it might be Barb and hurried to open it. To my surprise, several people were standing outside. My three elves, Mable, Ann, and Barb, as well as Alex Campbell and his wife Ruth from down the street greeted me. They all had their hands full of something. Mabel and Ann both had beautifully wrapped packages; Mabel was holding the top of a clothes hanger with what appeared to be a suit hanging under it, it was wrapped in a most joyful Christmas paper; Ann had a package beautifully decorated; and even Barb's offering was wrapped in Christmas paper. Alex seemed to have camera equipment, and I immediately remembered that he was a very qualified amateur photographer.

I ushered them all into the house, and they made themselves comfortable. Sarah brought in an assortment of the special cookies she usually bakes only at Christmas time along with a big bowl of eggnog. This was going to be a Christmas party!

There were the usual introductions, and then Sarah took the role of hostess. Through a trickling of tears she said, "Thank you all for coming. You are dear friends, and we love to have you with us to join in this marvelous occasion. Before we forget, thank you all for your contribution to make what we're doing possible. Everything is so much more meaningful when you have friends involved. As you know, we have decided to start off on a new venture in our lives. Robert has been so dear to me that I wanted him to have the very best, and that's why you're here."

She then turned to me and said, "Robert, we are ready to turn you into a new man. You couldn't get any better, so we just decided to dress you for what you are—a kind, loving, and giving person. We're merely going to dress you as what you have personified all your life."

With that, she gave me Mabel's package. I tore open the wrapping as eagerly as any kid would on Christmas morning. I knew it would be the suit, but I never could have been ready for what I saw. I had never felt the emotions I was now feeling. There my Santa suit was in all its glory. The only thing that came to my mind was a statement from the Bible—but with a slight change in the wording: *Consider Robert in his Santa suit; even Solomon in all his glory was not arrayed like this.* There was no *I wonder how I'll look in this* or *I hope I won't feel silly.* I just wanted to put it on and be Santa the rest of my life.

The moment was, to say the least, more than I had ever expected. It was as if no one else was in the room—just me and the suit. Where did they find all of these bits and pieces? The suit even had real golden buttons with little reindeer images on them. I counted them, eight in all, each bearing the name of one of Santa's reindeer. I thought to myself, *If I ever forget a reindeer's name, all I'll have to do is look down at the buttons.* I marveled at the gold-thread stitching. And I couldn't imagine where they found fur so white that it put snow to shame. It was real, and

I couldn't stop stroking it. The belt was real leather about four inches wide and polished to a brilliant shine. I wondered where they found such a large gold buckle.

My reverie was interrupted when Ann, not able to wait any longer, handed me another somewhat large package. I tore off the paper and found that several assorted-size boxes had been wrapped and packed inside the large package. I started with the smallest, which revealed a perfect set of gold-rimmed Santa glasses. I put them on, and they rested perfectly on the end of my nose. They were clear glass, and I could see through them perfectly.

The next box surprised me. It had six perfectly embroidered handkerchiefs that had the monogram *SC* beautifully sewn in one of the corners. Mabel said, "Well we couldn't just have you pull out any old hanky on a cold winter night."

Ann spoke up, "You'll probably be wiping more tears than your own," which turned out to be quite insightful. I was moved; they had thought of everything.

The next box was a handsome pair of hand-knitted mittens and a perfect Santa hat with the same white fur around the base and topped again with a ball of white fur right at its peak. The final box revealed a sturdy pair of black leather boots just the right height on the leg, the leather folded over at the top and the perfect size to accept a large pair of red woolen stockings that were stuffed in them.

And then, there it was—a most beautiful, large red Santa's bag perfect in every respect. It was tied with a large golden cord. I looked inside, and they had sewn a pouch that would hold necessary paperwork I might need. I could see that the bag would serve as Santa's briefcase. Inside the pouch was a very small, business-card-size, duplicate Santa bag. They had really thought ahead. Each item brought the hoped-for happy response. I was ready.

Hugs of love were in order, and Mabel and Ann received them graciously. I'd say we might have been a little overly emotional, but then I asked myself, *If such emotion is love, can we ever be overly emotional?* Obviously, a great mutual admiration was going on.

Barb handed me her package and said, "I hope you'll like this." Inside was a perfect presentation package with art layout for letterhead, envelopes, and business cards, choices of paper stock on each, and an appreciation or thank-you card.

Barb said, "I just thought the thank-you card would be a nice touch." Even on the job she had always gone the extra mile. She said, "Your wife called me and told me what was going on. I so wanted to be a part of it, and I am so glad I came."

Unlike most Christmas offerings with decorated trees, snowmen, holly, wreaths, and so forth, Barb had designed an uncluttered presentation. Exquisitely designed lettering declared that Santa doesn't need embellishments; he can stand on his own. All products carried the same message. At the top of the page, *Santa Claus* was printed in the left corner. Along the bottom of the card and letterhead she had written, *Can be reached locally at PO Box 1225*, and that was followed by the phone number. It was perfect.

Santa Claus

Can be reached locally at PO Box 1225 or call Local Number 842-667-7656

It probably would have taken me hours trying to choose little cutesy things that detracted from the message, which was, *You're dealing with Santa himself.* It wasn't difficult for Barb to see how pleased I was because I had a smile from one side on my face to the other. She said, "Is it okay?"

I reminded Barb of an advertising campaign we had done for a client at one time when we determined one approach would work okay. "Remember your remarks?" I asked. "Okay is adequate, tolerable, and suitable—but never good enough. Okay is average, we should never call ourselves average. Average is the best of the worst and the worst of the best. Barb, this is the best of the best. No Santa's helper has ever done it better."

In reality, my Christmas had come early. What's more, I got everything I had asked for and more. I felt almost unworthy of even putting the suit on, but with a lot of encouragement, I retired to the bedroom and carefully and respectfully dressed. Of course Sarah was right there to help me. Each time I put on an item, she handed me the next piece. I took time to look into our dressing mirror and admire myself as each piece was added. I couldn't believe how perfectly everything fit; they hadn't taken one measurement during the whole sewing process!

Once fully dressed, I viewed myself in the mirror behind the door. The only thing lacking was my fully grown beard, but after only two weeks of growth, it didn't look too bad. It was as though the suit were magical. I said to myself, *Just wearing it will make me wiser, happier, more giving, kinder, and respected.*

I was ready to make my first entrance as Santa. I sent Sarah into the other room, gave her time to get settled, and then walked out of the bedroom and into the living room. The reactions couldn't have been better. Jaws dropped, smiles appeared, and laughter flowed freely. Those reactions invoked laughter from the very depths of my soul, and I swear that from then on I never again had a problem with a Santa laugh. All were excited to be a part of the team and enjoyed the celebration of the beginning of this undertaking. I was so moved by what the mere presence of Santa could do to even a group like this.

I knew then that this was going to be a life-changing experience. The old Robert was now reborn as Santa, and I felt authenticated. I asked for a moment to say something, and the silence was immediate. I still remember vividly my discovery of the fact that when Santa speaks, people listen. I had only one thing I wanted to say, and I realized that my elves and I were hearing it for the first time. I said, "As long as I live, from this day forward, there'll always be a real Santa Claus." And then I thought to myself, *I may not affect many people, but to those I come in contact with, I'll be real.*

I found out that Sarah had mentioned to Mabel and Ann earlier that I had to have picture of me in the Santa suit. Ann, with her abundance of knowledge, recommended Alex. Alex had won several photo contest and had always been the type of neighbor that would do anything for anyone. His enthusiasm was indicative of his love for his profession.

Alex had his camera set up, and we started taking pictures. Everyone wanted a picture taken with Santa. Of course Mabel had to sit on one knee and Ann on the other, which was a good test to see if Santa's knees could hold up. We had a good time joking about that. After several publicity-type pictures had been taken, the evening was complete. Everyone left, and Sarah and I sat down to have a few quiet moments together and to let our love deepen. I realized that this was probably the last quiet moment we would have between then and Christmas.

4

Securing Employment

The next morning, the first thing I did was to look at my suit again to make sure it was real, and then I started on a very full day. Alex had given me the chip out of his camera, so I ran to Walmart and put it in the scanner and was amazed at the high quality of each shot. I had a few laughs at the joy on each face and at how proud I looked in my Santa suit. I picked my five favorite pictures and ordered five 8 1/2 by 11 copies of each. I then selected my favorite among the five and ordered 25 four by six copies of it for mailing purposes. I was told I could pick everything up later that afternoon.

From there, I hopped in the car and ran over to Office Max to pick up the publicity flyers they had printed for me. They looked better than I had anticipated. Everything was coming together so perfectly that I felt like it was probably meant to be. I left the carefully designed business card, letterhead, envelope, and thank-you card with the printing center at Office Max after ordering a sufficient quantity to get started as well as enough to see me through the forthcoming mass mailing. I was told I could pick up everything later that afternoon. I seemed to have a little more lift to my step and flew from one chore to the other.

Always in the back of my mind, I was a little fearful that I would go to all this work and put my friends to so much trouble and then not get many engagements. I would know the next day; it was my plan to visit the three malls and several companies. I would have all my materials by then and thought I could make a good presentation. At the time I went back to Walmart to pick up my pictures, I also picked up a great appointment book to keep a schedule of all my visits. It was small and leather bound and had plenty of room for the data I would need to record— names, addresses; telephone numbers, appointment times, contact information, and so forth. It would fit perfectly in my Santa bag pouch. I was ready.

Later that day, after I had picked up the things from Office Max and the pictures from Walmart, I headed home. I laid out everything on the kitchen table and gave them one last inspection. I had everything ready, and the whole process had taken me only two weeks.

I went to bed early that night. That didn't do me a lot of good because I was just like a kid on Christmas Eve. It was impossible to go to sleep. I rehearsed over and over again what I would say on each appointment. I went through all kinds of scenarios: *I'm sorry the boss can't see you now*; *We already have our Santa*; *Just leave your information, and I'll see it gets to the right person*; *What do you have to offer that's different from the other Santa's?*

I knew that the hardest part of any sales job was getting to the right person; I also knew that a little kind persistence often enabled this. Once in front of the right person, I knew it was important to have all the correct answers and materials. I felt like saying, *Do you think Santa has all the time in the world? It's Christmas! I'm a busy man. Do you want me to put you on my naughty list?* What I decided to say was, "This is a pretty busy time of the year for me; I'd surely appreciate it if I could just have five minutes of the manager's time. I have new ideas for a mall Santa, and I think he might like to hear them." I had worked so hard in my mind on each presentation that I knew I would find it quite easy to be convincing when I arrived at the different offices.

My first visit was at the Downtown Mall. I had done my homework and knew that Mr. Burgess was the person I should talk with. As I opened the door and walked in, a buzzer was tripped and a lady stood up and peered over a cubicle wall. She said, "Yes?" There was no "May I help you?" Just "Yes?" I asked to see Mr. Burgess and was told to go down the hall, first office on the left.

When I reached the office, the door was open, so I took a step in. A short but very pleasant-looking fellow said, "Hello."

I told him I was looking for Mr. Burgess, and he confirmed that I had found him. He asked what he could do for me, and I presented him with one of my cards and informed him I was there to apply to be the mall's Santa Claus. I was surprised at his question, "Do you have references?"

I had never taken this need into consideration, I was quick to recover, though. I always thought honesty to be the best policy and said, "I have none as yet, and this will be my first employment as Santa."

He informed me of how careful the mall has to be these days and said it would be hard to hire anyone without references or experience. I told him I could get many good personal references, and I pointed out that even Santa had to have a first job somewhere. He laughed a little and said, "Yes I suppose so. What are your qualifications?"

I had all my qualifications uppermost in my mind because I had recently included them on my resume. I merely stated that I had worked the last thirty-five years as the manager of the public relations department for a very large company. I then told him that after thirty-five years of facing public problems and putting out many fires, I still loved people very much. He seemed to agree with me that this was a significant qualification but said he would still need references. I assured him I would have several for him very shortly. He then made a statement that I thought quite humorous when he said, "Well, you're certainly about the right age."

He asked me if I had my own Santa suit. When I presented him with my several pictures, I could see immediately that he was very impressed. I told him my beard was still in its growing stages but would be very presentable by the time it was needed. He seemed impressed enough with it and said, "Don't grow it too long. I like a Santa with a full but controlled beard."

He paused for a minute and then threw in the only damper of our whole conversation. He said, "We have had the same Santa every year for the last five years. We probably owe him a little allegiance because he's been such a good Santa. Before I commit myself, I think I owe it to him to discuss his availability again."

He said that they had had some problems with Santas missing several days because of illness last year. When I told him I'd missed only three days of work in the last thirty-five years, he seemed quite impressed. He then gave me a little hope when he said, "He has usually contacted us by now, but we haven't heard from him as yet." I was told that I should get some references together and that they would certainly consider my request.

I thanked him very much and told him that it might take me a couple of days to get the proper references but that he could certainly expect me back. As I shook his hand and turned to leave, he said, "Oh, by the way, our last Santa provided his own photographer. Do you have one in mind?"

Until then, my thinking had been that the mall people would want their own photographer as another source of funds to help offset the cost of a Santa. That's why I hadn't considered or approached anyone to be Santa's photographer. Of course

Alex came to my mind first. I couldn't remember what he did for a living. I *had* thought about Santa photographers, though. In my mind, photographers seemed to relegate Santa to a mere prop, a Christmas backdrop, a Christmas setting rather than a viable person with a purpose. I told Mr. Burgess that. And then I pointed out that I was interested in making Santa an experience and that I wanted his visitors to remember the man and not the picture because pictures just find their way into a drawer anyway and are seldom ever brought out to look at. After I mentioned this concept to Mr. Burgess, I was surprised at his immediate grasp of the situation.

I told him that nothing should come between the child and Santa because any distraction would reduce the child's connection to the wonders of Christmas. I was quick to add that this didn't mean the parents couldn't take their own pictures; almost all people now carried a camera with them wherever they went, especially because so many cell phones could function as a camera. I suggested a posting a sign that would read, *Please feel free to take candid pictures.* My plan would literally make photographers out of parents, brothers and sisters, aunts and uncles, and even friends.

In the past, I had seen photographers almost get into fights with patrons because patrons were taking pictures of the photographers' perfectly posed subjects. Naturally, the photographers thought that if patrons had their own pictures, they wouldn't order any from the photographers. I had also heard of people who didn't take their kids to see Santa because it was just too expensive.

For myself, I wanted the freedom to stand up and sit down because if the lines got too long, I could make them shorter by just walking around to hurry the process. And I didn't want to have to remain stationary just so I wouldn't be out of the photographer's focus. I made the point that I would never neglect a single child. In fact I could probably give them more time if I didn't have to sit and wait for them to come to me and be posed. Besides, nobody likes a line at Christmas time.

I had been so busy going over all of these reasons for not having a photographer that I hadn't looked up to see the big smile on Mr. Burgess's face. Not wanting to leave anything to chance, I told him I considered it my job to get more people into his mall and then help them to enjoy it once they were there. I assured him that I would know where every store in the mall was located and what each store offered. I pointed out that all these details were important so I could direct people to the gift they requested for Christmas. I was already having fun and felt very adequate.

Mr. Burgess grasped my situation fully; he seemed to know that I needed a commitment and asked if I had looked elsewhere. I told him I planned on visiting all three malls in the city today. He assured me that the moment he had my references I would have an answer. He asked me if I would give him first right of refusal. I thought that fair and told him so. He said, "You must understand that if I were to hire you without references and then something went wrong, I would be criticized for not doing my job correctly." How well I knew his plight.

It wasn't difficult to see why Mr. Burgess had been chosen for his position. He was professional in every respect but also was very pleasant to work with. I envisioned a good relationship between us, so I put him on my "nice list." *That's funny*, I said to myself. *Mentally, I've started making both naughty and nice lists, but I haven't listed even one person as 'naughty' yet.*

I chose to go to this mall first because it had always been my favorite. The experience with Mr. Burgess had been so satisfactory that I decided to put off visits to the other two malls and settle for now with my visit to the Downtown Mall and some visits to businesses. And then with a certain amount of surprise I realized that money had never been mentioned. I guess neither of us wanted, at the time, to relegate Santa to a monetary figure.

I had several large companies on my list of daily visits. I chose the one nearest to where I was and headed that way. On the way, I passed a very pleasant-looking office building with a sign in the front that read, *The Olaf Company*. Without knowing why, I found myself pulling into their parking lot. I grabbed one of my promotional packets and began walking toward the building.

Once inside, I easily determined that this was a successful company. Everything in the foyer was immaculately chosen and strategically placed. I was well within the building before I reached the receptionist desk. There were two receptionists; I could easily tell they were chosen because of their cordial personalities, which seemed to be exceeded only by their intelligence. I was asked if I had an appointment, and I stayed in line with their demeanor and declared I needed their help to determine the right person with whom to talk. Upon being told that they would be pleased to help, I stated my purpose for being there and then handed each of them a business card.

They looked at each other for clarification and for a moment didn't seem to have an answer. After a brief discussion and a strategically placed phone call, they told me I probably should talk to Ms. Geldenhuys. I asked if I might see her and was told to have a seat in the foyer while they contacted her office. A very short time later an elevator door opened and a young lady stepped out and walked toward me. She thanked me for waiting and assured me that Ms. Geldenhuys was the proper person to talk to about being a Santa. She then said, "Ms. Geldenhuys asked if you could leave what information you have so she can look it over and give you a call."

In response, I said, "There's so much that printed literature and pictures cannot tell about choosing the right Santa, and I'm sure you'll agree that your company deserves the best Santa. Is there some way I could please have five minutes of her time?"

I was told she was in a meeting and couldn't meet with me for at least an hour. I told her I would be glad to return in an hour and made note of the time. I thanked her, and she whispered to me, "I just made an executive decision; I hope I don't get in trouble."

I returned in an hour and was happy to see that Ms. Geldenhuys honored the decision of her assistant. I was taken to the third floor and was shown into a very spacious office that definitely reflected a woman's embellishments.

The assistant introduced me to Ms. Geldenhuys as the vice president of public affairs. She greeted me very cordially, as if I *were* the real Santa, and then asked the impish question, "*Are you the real Santa?*"

In a truthful manner, I declared that I was. She laughingly played with me, stating, "I have always believed in you."

I answered her by saying, "Thank you, you've always been on my nice list."

We were off to a good start. I explained to her that I specialized in being Santa for company parties and could adapt well to any situation. She told me my timing was impeccable because she had just been given the assignment to find a Santa for this year's gala. She mentioned that she had been told to pick just the right employee, rent him a good outfit, and go over a good night's agenda with him. She asked me the kind of question I thought a company officer should ask: "Why should we hire an outside Santa over an inside Santa?"

She knew I'd know what she meant. I handed her my best Santa picture and said, "This is the main reason. You can't hire a suit of clothes like this."

I then handed her a standard picture of a Santa in a rented suit that I had earlier cut out of a rental magazine, and said, "This is one of the best rented suits—if you can get it to fit this well."

She adjusted her glasses for a perfect look and said, "Oh my, I see what you mean."

I went on to tell her that a professional Santa most often could be hired for less money than a company would have to spend to rent a complete Santa outfit. She assured me that cost had nothing to do with it; most of all, they wanted to have a good party. I added that a good party is made better with a good Santa. She responded, "Yes, but someone from inside the company can have fun with the employees with little bits of inside information they may be privy to."

I told her that inside information sometimes led to outside uneasiness and then added, "Unless it comes from a third party who is not an employee."

She got the picture fast. I told her that with just the right information about several company members, we could have a lot of fun. Part of my life's training had given me the capability to discern where to draw the line between a good joke and a hurtful experience. I then ended it by asking how many really good Santa's had come from company employees. She just looked at me and said, "I'm sold; how long do you need on the program?"

I told her that was her decision but let her know that it shouldn't be dragged out too long but that a good Santa should be able to accomplish his purpose in a half hour to forty-five minutes. This response interested her, and she asked, "Just what is the purpose of a good Santa?"

I answered her that a good Santa's purpose should be to bring the spirit of Christmas to the party and set the tone for the night's celebration.

Once again, I never brought up the costs for the night. To be truthful, dollar amounts hadn't crossed my mind thus far in the conversation. Almost as if to change the subject, she said, "Will a hundred dollars cover your expenses for the night?

After a short hesitation, I told her that would do. I was given the date of the party and my arrival time and asked if I needed any props, such as a large chair. I told her a large chair would be nice, along with some sort of sound system. I agreed to bring everything else of a "props" nature that was needed for the night. She thanked me for making her job a lot easier, which I noted as another good reason for future reference. We parted company feeling good about each other. She stopped me as I was about halfway out of her office and asked, "Do we need any kind of contract or paperwork?"

I said, "Do you trust Santa? I already know I can trust you; you're on my nice list."

She laughed and said, "See you at the party."

As I walked out to the car, I made a mental note to draw up a simple contract in case I needed one in the future. And then I asked myself two questions: *Does Santa really need protection? Is there anyone out there who would cheat on Santa?*

It was midafternoon. I decided to stop at one more business and then get home to work on references and to draw up a contract.

At the final visit of the day, I was told that the owner of the company, the boss, always plays Santa at the company party and that there was no reason for pursuing my Santa interests. I told the person I was talking to that I could compete with almost anyone but the boss. I thanked him for his time and got up to leave. He said under his breath, "I wish someone could convince him to get another Santa. He's not very good at it."

I gave him my card and said, "Give this to the boss; I'll follow up later."

I made a note of my visit and left.

When I got home, Sarah greeted me at the door and said, "You're home sooner than I thought. Didn't it go well?"

I told her I had met with only three people. "One said "no," one said "maybe," and one said 'yes.'"

That didn't quite register with her. She had prepared herself for the worst, so any positive result was out of place. When it did register, she didn't know how to react. She didn't know whether to laugh or cry. We settled for a big celebration hug, and she insisted on hearing every last word. I told her every detail because she deserved to know everything. It was fun to watch her enthusiasm. When I finished, the questions started flying: "Do you think you have a good chance at the mall job? How much is the company that hired you going to pay?

When I told her the amount, $100, it was as if she had struck gold. I decided to tell her I planned to go back to the company that said no and tell the boss, in a respectful way, that the employees wanted a new Santa. She laughed out loud. She got up and started walking out of the room. I asked her where she was going, and she said, "I've got to call Mabel and Ann. They'll be so happy with the good news."

Before it got much later in the day, I started my next telephone campaign, which was calling several people to request character references from them. My first call was to Joe, my old boss. I said, "Joe, don't be surprised, but I think I've found new employment and I need a character reference,"

He replied, "Say no more. I'll have one faxed over to you within the hour. What's the job anyway?"

I told him I was applying for the job as Santa for a local mall. He gave a skeptical laugh and said, "I'll call Jordan for you and get him to send over a reference also. Just go tend to your reindeer and I'll see that this gets done."

I called a lady for whom I had headed up a service project, and then I called the bishop of my church. By that night, I had four references and wondered who this great guy was they were talking about in their reference letters.

I had drawn up a few contracts in my day, and found myself getting quite technical in the terms I was using. I thought, *If I had my way, we would do it on a handshake anyway. I certainly don't intend to take advantage of anyone, and if someone takes advantage of me, which is very unlikely, I'd merely be out of an hour's work. Besides, I won't sign with my real name—I'll just sign as Santa.* I ended up preparing a simple agreement:

To the _____ Company

It is agreed that Santa will provide his services on _____, beginning at _____ AM / PM and ending at _____ AM / PM. For these services, it is agreed that he will receive the sum of $_____.

Signature _____
Santa Claus

Company Signature _____

Before retiring, I sat up for a few minutes and pondered the day I had just had. I kind of felt that more was going on than meets the eye. Being able to just walk into Mr. Burgess's office was too easy, and pulling into the Olaf Company parking lot was almost too much of a coincidence. In fact, the way I became a Santa was beyond my explanation. *Maybe there's a Santa Claus up there looking out for me,* I thought. I would find out as I went along with this Santa chapter of my life that there would be many unexplained incidents of the kind that I think of as miracles. I decided just to go along with any promptings that might come my way.

5

Santa Successes

My first order of business the next morning was to make several copies of my references and my Santa contract. I laughed when I reread the contract because it sounded more like an appointment reminder. I added these items to my Santa packets. Next, I completed one of the thank-you notes to Ms. Geldenhuys to confirm the agreement we had reached, put it in an envelope, and decided to deliver it by hand later in the day. Next, I pulled out my new appointment book and carefully wrote under December 14 at 7:00PM, *Olaf Company, contact: Ms. Geldenhuys.* This was my very first entry, and I did it with somewhat of a flare.

I then went through my morning routine by having my drink and toast, reading the news and sports in the newspaper, and getting cleaned up and dressed for the day. I had a little more time than usual. I really couldn't start my visits until after 10:00AM; this would give people time to settle in. I decided to mail several promotional flyers to test the market. I thought twenty would be sufficient. The mailer consisted of a flyer and one of my Santa pictures. After addressing them, I placed Santa stamps on them that I had picked up from the Post Office. I inserted a flyer and a picture of me, and believed that both were good enough to draw attention and attract inquiries.

I got to thinking about the Downtown Mall and Mr. Burgess. I was sure he would require a more inclusive contract than my simple document. I thought of ways to keep my anonymity and not have to reveal my real name but couldn't imagine their not wanting a contract made legal by address and signature. A thought came to me—why not use a separate restrictive agreement? I could have a one-page document drawn up that would restrict them from giving my real name and contact information to any other party. This could be attached to their contract as an addendum and would give me the privacy I required. For the life of me, I didn't know why I was so adamant on this point, but I reasoned that because I felt so strongly about it, there must be a legitimate rationale behind it. I thought the explanation would come to me later and put it to rest.

Once again I relied on past associations and called Barry Brown, who had headed up the legal department in our company. I told him what I was doing and what I needed, and he agreed to get right on it. He was working for a law firm now and told me he would have to charge a fee for the document to be ethical, but he assured me that the document already existed in his law files, that he merely would have to insert names, and that the whole package wouldn't be very costly. I gave him the go-ahead and was told he couldn't get it done until tomorrow. I was sure other contracts couldn't be put together that fast, so I told him that would be fine. He then said, "Because you're going to be a Santa, maybe we could work the fee out through a Santa visit. I'll see what I can do."

I left the house about 10:30AM and went straight to the Olaf Company to deliver my thank-you note to Ms. Geldenhuys. I went into the lobby, walked up to the two receptionists, and said, "Hi Mary and Alice. Will you see that Ms. Geldenhuys gets this, please?"

Mary took the card and said, "Yes, but how do you know our names?"

I said, "Well I *am* Santa aren't I?" And then I added, "Oh, and by the way, let your son Mikey and your daughter Riley know that I'll be to your home on Christmas Eve." I had gathered the names and information from Ms. Geldenhuys' assistant before leaving after my original trip; I thought it would make a fun touch.

After a stop at a nearby Post Office to mail the fliers and copies of my favorite Santa picture that Alex had taken, I headed back to the Downtown Mall. I was feeling a little hesitant in having this meeting with Mr. Burgess. It wasn't my nature to put things off, but there was a little fear of a negative response. I thought to myself, *I need a shot of confidence.*

I gathered up my materials and, as Santa, went boldly forward. Mr. Burgess was not reserved at all in his enthusiastic greeting. He said, "I was going to call you this afternoon. There's a lot we have to work out. First of all, I want to give you full rein to be the kind of Santa you want to be. This means you'll have the freedom to implement the programs you think will best serve the mall for Christmas. I talked it over with mall management, and we came to the conclusion that Santa should be able to be himself." He then said, "Oh, by the way, you made me look good." And then, as an afterthought, he said, "Oh, you *will* take the position, won't you? We want to make Santa the center of all Christmas promotions this year."

I told him that of course I would be the mall's Santa and that I would be the kind of Santa the mall management wanted. I somewhat hesitantly handed him my folder with all the references in it. He invited me into his office to temporarily work out all the details. I watched as he placed the files I had given him in the bottom drawer of a file cabinet. He asked me if we could wait to talk about finances until we had determined the nature of the work. I agreed and felt good that the details would not be influenced by the cost but that the costs would be influenced by the amount and type of work involved.

Scheduling was first. I was told that the mall was always closed on Sunday, which was fine with me. I expressed my admiration for that policy. He told me that they would like to have me for the other six days of each week. This would involve about six weeks of work, and I didn't feel that would be more than I could endure. I'd be required to work eight hours daily from 10:00AM to 6:00PM. With their experience, they had determined it to be too costly to pay for more hours, and the majority of the people shopped between those times. This pleased me to no end because I could still cover two to three Christmas parties each night. When he gave me the starting and ending dates, I told him I definitely couldn't work Christmas Eve day. He asked why not and I said, "Well it's pretty obvious isn't it? I have a lot of visits to make that night, and I don't think children would want to see Santa at the mall when he should be getting ready to make his Christmas visits." He smiled and chuckled.

They would provide a beautiful Santa village right in the center of the mall. He asked if I needed an elf and then alluded to the fact that the manager's daughter was attending school at a nearby college and would be available for six hours each day. They of course would put her on their payroll. He then assured me that she would be a great elf. I agreed with one stipulation— that my elves and I would provide the elf costume she would wear. He was delighted with this.

He then mentioned that they would provide the candy canes. I stopped him right there and said, "Have you ever seen a young person walking down the mall after he or she has eaten a candy cane?" We agreed that they should reconsider and maybe come up with an alternative.

Then Mr. Burgess (I hadn't found out his first name yet) said, "Let's determine a budget."

That suggestion prompted several thoughts to run through my mind. I know that malls get a basic rental fee from each store location and a bonus when certain grosses are exceeded. All stores more than exceed their minimums at Christmas, so malls collect good bonuses at this time of year. On top of this, about forty kiosks are added at the rental cost of up to $5,000 a month for November and December, so the malls aren't hurting.

However, I reminded myself that I didn't want to barter prices, so I thought I would sit back and let Mr. Burgess suggest a fee. I did tell him that I wasn't the bartering type. "If you have a limit, just let me know; and I'll see if I can live with it."

He said, "Well I know what we've paid in the past, but I'm also aware of what we got in the past. Oh, by the way, we did try to contact last year's Santa, and his phone was disconnected." Then he added, "I won't insult you with a low bid and then raise it if I have to; I'll just flat out tell you the top line of what we've budgeted for a Santa, and I hope it'll be acceptable."

He then gave me the figure of $7,000 for the season. A quick calculation for 204 hours gave me $35 per hour, much less than the hundred per hour at a party but guaranteed work. Without sounding overly eager, I told him I could make that work, and we shook hands on it. We both agreed that there might have to be a little tweaking as outside factors were brought to our attention. However, in general terms, we agreed. He stated he would have a contract ready for me Monday. I told him about my addendum for anonymity. He said that would not be a problem, and we were both satisfied. I agreed to meet him Monday when he would show me the plans for the Santa setting and acquaint me with the mall operations. He invited me to lunch at the food court; we went down and had lunch at Chick-Fil-A, which was on the house when the manager found out who I was. We had a wonderful, friendly conversation, and I found out that Mr. Burgess' first name was Martin—Martin Burgess.

I thought to myself, *I'd better go home and enter each date in my calendar before I start setting up any other appointments.* As I was driving home, I noted that I had now taken care of Mrs. Field's Christmas and then some. I was very satisfied with myself.

When I arrived home, I found Sarah out on the back patio putting the flowerbeds to rest for the winter. I said, "We're going to need an elf suit for a young lady." I could picture images of elves going through her head. She started asking about sizes, colors, elf shoes, and so forth, and then it hit her. "You got the job!"

I laughed and nodded in the affirmative. I've learned to brace myself for what's coming when Sarah celebrates a success—hugs and kisses and tears. "Oh, I knew you would."

That was all she said, but it was enough. Then came questions that took me about half an hour to answer. Not once did she ask what I would be paid; the position was all that was important to her. She ran to the phone, and I went back to work. I filled in my calendar and started making my party plans. There were nineteen party days in December if companies had their parties as early as December 1. I could probably fit several parties in per night. I could start as early as 6:30PM, although I realized that most of them would start at 7:00PM or maybe at 8:00PM or 8:30PM. So I reasoned that I could manage only 38 parties for the season with just two parties a night. It didn't seem like too big of an order. And if I could fit in three parties each night, I would have to find only 57 companies that wanted a Santa.

I left a little early the next morning to get some more pictures printed because both Mr. Burgess and Ms. Geldenhuys wanted to keep the ones I had shown them. I had decided at this point that a mass mailing would be appropriate, so I also ordered the quantity of smaller pictures needed to cover such an undertaking. I had made a list of the large companies located closest to the mall because I realized that easy access would save me time and because I would be able to attend more parties by reducing driving time. I had also decided, after my experience with the Olaf Company, to keep my eyes open for companies I may have missed when doing my research. I smiled to myself as I reflected that the pop-in method seemed to work.

After my first five visits, I was unsuccessful in booking a single party. Two companies took packets for consideration; two other companies told me they had their parties in the office during the day when I couldn't be there; and the fifth was almost a humbug situation: "We give a good bonus. Most people don't have time for parties at this time of year anyway. We can't seem to find a time that suits everyone." I felt sorry for the group as a whole.

Once outside, I took out my appointment book. In the back of the book on a page I had labeled *Needs Santa's Help*, I wrote down the company name.

By the end of the day, I had found two companies that thought my role as their Santa was a wonderful idea; they would have to get approval from higher up but thought it should be no problem. I made two appointments to return and talk to the decision makers. Three companies weren't at all interested, and one company scheduled a party for December 1, which thrilled me to get one that early in the month. To no one but myself, I said out loud, "Two appointments, one mall contract, and several possibilities aren't bad for the first few days."

The company that agreed to my visit caused another concern I had to consider. When we arrived at the point of discussing costs, they told me that they had had Santa's for the last several years and had paid them $125 and didn't want to go much over that. Of course I was ready to accept their offer, but the thought came to me, *Do I need to have a standard fee for all clients?* I could just hear the conversation between two companies that do business together. "How was your Christmas? We had a great party and one of the best Santa's ever. He charged us only $100." After a few comparisons, they would find out both of them had the same Santa, but the one paying $125 would seem somewhat cheated. I thought, *Santa can't make people feel bad.* I needed to think this one over so I just said, "That would be fine, and I can make it work." I thought that I could always come back later and lower the price.

As usual, I reported my day to Sarah. She was excited. I discussed my dilemma regarding the charges for each party. She stated that this was a business decision and was out of the realm of her expertise. But then she said, "I do suppose it could be kind of a 'what's the decent thing to do problem,' couldn't it?" Little did she know that she had taken it out of the business arena and placed it in the realm of ethics? Whether it was okay to charge a higher price to one company just because its leaders couldn't bargain as well as someone else just became out of the question. My code of conduct just wouldn't allow it. Because I agreed on $100 for the first company, all companies would retain my services at the bargain price of $100.

I had only four and a half weeks left to make 38 to 57 appointments. Realizing that, I noted the need to make a minimum of two appointments a day for the next twenty-four days to even get close to my goals. I decided that I might as well make a mass mailing to the remaining companies. I thought to myself, *If I do a mass mailing on Friday, the recipients should receive them Monday or Tuesday, and I should start hearing back on Wednesday or Thursday.* I spent the rest of the evening getting the mailing ready.

The next morning before I got out the door, my Santa cell phone rang. Because no one else had the number but those I had contacted, I knew it would be a business call. My first thought was, *I hope it's not someone calling to cancel.* I answered, "Santa."

The pleasant female voice on the other end of the line said, "I'm so excited! I've never talked to Santa on the phone before."

Then she gave a little giggle. She introduced herself as Marcia Foster with the Montrose Company. "I understand you've been chatting with Bernadette Geldenhuys, who told me you're a wonderful Santa. We're having a party on December 7, and we're wondering if we could secure your services."

I told her to hold on while I consulted my appointment calendar. I took just enough time for that purpose and then assured her that date would be acceptable. She said that Bernadette had told her the cost and that it was $100. "Is that right?"

We spoke for a while, and I told her I would like to come by and meet her and gather some relevant information. She said, "I can't wait to meet you."

I told her I would call in about a week for an appointment, and we left it at that.

I don't mean to go on and on with every single story that happened, but they're all worth telling. Some of them should be told if for no other reason than to strengthen the rest of us. For instance, upon approaching one company, I was taken in and introduced to one of their executives. He knew my purpose for being there and asked if I would mind if he could just tell me something. I told him, "Of course not," and then he asked if I was to be their Santa. When I told him I hoped so, he said, "Good, I had to know that I was talking directly to a Santa Claus." He then said, "This might seem a little strange at first, but I'll explain it to you later. Julie, she's my daughter, told me to tell you that you wouldn't have to bother about coming to her this year." He then said with some relief, "There, my job is done."

The explanation and his devotion to his daughter needs sharing. He told me that several months earlier, he and his wife found out that Julie had a rare cancer that would, in the end, take her life. They spent the time left with her doing things she had always wanted to do until she had no more strength to do them. One night he was reading her a story while she was cuddling her favorite little teddy bear. He asked her if she loved it, and she said, "Yes. Santa brought it to me last Christmas."

He said that she went completely quiet for a while, hugged her bear very, very close, and then said, "Daddy, when you see Santa, will you please tell him he won't have to come this year."

He then told me that she had passed away shortly afterward. I wanted to run right out and shout to every mother and father that they *must* love each precious minute they are given with their children.

6

Meeting My Elf

I continued to go about my daily calls. My beard was growing in properly, and every once in a while I'd try on the suit just to see its effect. My calendar was filling in much faster than I thought it would. By the 16th of November, I had all the appointments I could handle. I had forty-eight party appointments. As things turned out, I probably could have added a few more but decided to leave a few extra spots just in case there might be a last-minute need or maybe Santa might be prompted to call on someone unexpectedly. I had many direct calls from my mailings, several referrals, and a few appointments from direct visits.

I decided to spend the rest of the time before Thanksgiving visiting the rest of the businesses that engaged me so I could gather pertinent information to be used at each party. I prepared a list of questions in case my contacts needed prompting as to facts about their business. The list went something like this:

1. Who in the company has recently been promoted?

2. Who has recently been engaged or wants to be?

3. Who has been employed by the company the longest?

4. Who is the youngest employee?

5. Who is the oldest employee?

6. What other fun information can you share about the company, goofs by management or employees, funny company customs, unique company routines or practices, company successes, etc.?

I was motivated by my thinking: *The more information gathered, the more meaningful the party.*

I should add here that I enjoyed every minute of the work I was doing. I was meeting new people every day under the most pleasant of circumstances. When we associate with people while they are at their best, it's a pleasant experience.

I was to meet with Martin Burgess at the mall the next day to go over final plans and to meet my elf assistant. When I arrived, I was told that Haley, the elf girl, would be there in an hour, which gave us time to walk the mall and see where I would be stationed. Right in the center of the mall was a big rotunda with a high circular dome where I was told my throne would be located. I asked, "*Throne?*"

Martin responded, "Certainly. You're the king of Christmas, so you deserve a place of dignity."

I said, "All I want is a comfortable place that will allow a lot of room for kids to gather around."

Martin replied, "That's exactly what we have in mind."

He then showed me an artist's rendering of the Santa setting. I was amazed; it was beautiful. My throne sat at the back of the arc, and there was a wide, circular path going around the outside of the circle. With each step, a child would get closer to Santa and would see another beautiful Christmas decoration. There were sugar-plum fairies, small reindeer, gaily clothed elves, gingerbread houses, large lollipops, candy canes, and so much more that I had a difficult time taking it all in. And there was a large, open circle with a big, plush red carpet right in the center and directly in front of the throne. The colors were vibrant, and the spirit was evident.

Every so often, there was a break in the path where parents could wander to the center of the circle and take pictures. All kinds of little animated animals popped out of holes or from behind logs or from tree limbs. I could see that children would be captivated and entertained from the moment they entered. For some unexplained reason, I started giving names to the animals. To top it all off, thousands of stars of different sizes hung at different heights from the rotunda, giving it a very mystical effect. I asked if I could take the drawing home to show Sarah and was told I could because they had other copies.

After giving it much thought, we determined that the children were used to getting candy canes and that most of them loved them. Candy canes seemed to be as much about Christmas as any of the alternatives we explored. Sarah had waylaid my fear of sticky children walking all over the mall by merely saying, "Most mothers are prepared for children messes. I don't think I know a mother who doesn't have a purse full of hand wipes." Martin assured me they would try to find some special candy canes that were, as he put it, "a little out of the ordinary."

It wasn't too long before a very delicate young lady showed up, and I was introduced to Haley, my elf. If I were producing a movie and had to rely on casting to get the right person for the part, they couldn't have done better. No, she didn't have pointed ears. Of course I never thought Santa's elves' ears were pointed anyway. She did have large perfect oval eyes, a small, flawlessly formed nose, and a smile that welcomed everyone. She had just turned twenty and hoped I didn't think she was too old. I asked her one question and received the answer I wanted, "Do you like children?" She excitedly replied, "I can't get enough of them."

She was majoring in music at the university. When I asked her why she chose music, she told me she played a flute and planned on making that her career. I later learned that she had earned a full-ride scholarship because of her talent. No one would have to be a genius to know what was going through my mind—an elf who plays the flute every once in a while to delight the throngs with one of the many carols of the season. I asked in a way that I hoped would not be too assuming what she thought about playing a carol periodically. She said she knew them all and would sincerely love to play them. "That's what we artists are all about, we love having an audience to play for."

We got down to discussing costumes, and she said, "The simpler the better, but I don't like curly-toed shoes."

She had been informed that we insisted on providing the elf costume, so she came prepared with all her measurements. When I showed her the picture of me in the Santa suit, she got really excited about being a part of the team. I collected her email address, phone number, and home address. As it turned out, we didn't live very far from each other. I told her we would call her the minute the costume was completed. I snapped a picture of her so Sarah could see the elf for whom she was sewing. I told her to come up with any ideas she might have to make this a great Christmas season, and she was delighted that I had put such trust in her. Martin was very happy that Haley and I got along so well and couldn't wait to get started.

Upon arriving home, I gave Haley's picture and measurements to Sarah. Her first words were, "Isn't she just the perfect little pixie. She'll have to have a very plain costume that won't detract from her natural beauty."

Interestingly, they had never met but had both agreed that the costume would have to be simple. Sarah had a picture in her mind, and she described it to me: "It must be green velvet; it must be short; it must have a round, fur collar and must have three round, white fur buttons spaced evenly from the collar to the waist; the sleeves should come down to her wrist and be edged with fur; the skirt should be slightly flared with white fur at the bottom; and it definitely has to be the same white fur that we used on the Santa suit. We'll give her green tights to match and a beautiful pair of black-patent, ballerina-type flat shoes. She must have a green hat just like Santa's red one, and she should have two braided pigtails because of the length of her hair."

She didn't wait for my reply but ran straight to the telephone. Before long, Mabel and Ann were sitting in the kitchen again looking at a sketch Sarah had drawn.

By the 14th of November the elf costume was completed. I called Haley to ask if she could come over and try it on. She asked if she could bring her parents, which we preferred anyway. It would give us a chance to meet them and get their total approval.

Mabel and Ann arrived with the elf outfit, and it wasn't much later that Haley and her parents joined us. The father, the mall manager, was very happy about the Christmas prospects for the mall, but other than that, he pointed out that any further conversation would just delay the elf presentation. Sarah handed Haley a nice dress box. She lifted the lid, and her smile lit up the whole room. It was just the right color. The fur was marvelous, and it was not the usual silly elf costume. With a cute smile, Haley said, "Thanks for not making me wear curly-toed shoes. Now where can I go to try everything on? And Santa, can we see you in your suit?" I liked the way she *always* called me Santa.

I went to our bedroom, Haley went to the guest bedroom, and we agreed to come out together when signaled. A few minutes later, Sarah said, "Are you ready?"

We both walked into the living room together. Well, I don't know what happened, but everybody just sat there and quietly stared at us. Nobody made a sound. We were told later after cheers and laughs that they were just too stunned to say anything.

We made a perfect pair, and one suit enhanced the other. Haley had no inhibitions; she flitted around the room as any proper elf would, and pure joy showed itself in her every action.

She then ran over and said to her mother, "Give me Freddy."

That's what she had named her flute. She wanted to play for us, and we were thrilled with her eagerness. She played a rendition of "Santa Claus Is Coming to Town" embellished with runs and trills, all suggesting how serious it was to take Santa for granted. She moved around with easiness as if to imply that the tune was directed to each one of us individually. It was, to say the least, enchanting. She was just what I wanted—an elf who could totally captivate everyone with her charm and personality.

After Mabel, Ann, and Sarah had admired their handy work, Haley refolded the costume with the loving care given to a prized possession. I could see right then why Santa cherished his elves. The next time I would see her would be at 10:00AM on November 23rd. She would be with me the whole day to kick things off right.

7

First Day on the Job

In the eight days left, I finished all my preparations, gathered all the needed information from the companies, visited the mall several times to check the progress, and reveled in the day-by-day wonderment of the soon-to-be Christmas season. People gathered around just to admire each addition. I visited the mall stores and with the help of employees, got a good idea of what each offered. I spent extra time at the toy store getting all the information needed. The manager, Mr. Henley, spent time walking each aisle with me to explain how each toy worked. He told me all their names and pointed out the most popular toys this year. I received a Dolls 101 course that served me well through the season. I felt like I learned more information about dolls than I knew about humans and wondered how any one person could get to know all there is to know about dolls—not to mention the accessories. I thought, *Santa Claus is probably the only person who knows all there is to know about dolls.* The degree of seriousness I was giving to this part of my education surprised even myself. I felt it very important to be knowledgeable about every aspect of being a Santa. I thought to myself, *I want to be in a position to never disappoint a single child.*

At night, I studied the information I had gathered on each company I was to visit and somewhat prepare myself as to what I was to say. I wanted each occasion to be as spontaneous as possible, and I knew that each party would provide its own opportunity for merriment. After all, Santa couldn't get up and read from notes.

My beard cooperated without a blemish; it was white as I had wished and was full and easy to manage. Mabel and Ann stopped by occasionally. They said they just wanted to see if there was anything more they needed to do, but I knew their true motives were to check on my beard. On one of their visits, Sarah wasn't there because she had gone after groceries. I asked them if they were up to doing another project for me, and we discussed it for quite a while. I told them not to mention it to anyone, especially Sarah.

It was Thanksgiving night and my tummy was full. Lately, I allowed myself to eat a little more than I had been used to eating. I'm not sure about my true feelings one day when Mabel blurted out, "Well, one good thing, Robert won't need any stuffing in his suit."

I was going over every item I could think of, trying to figure out whether I had forgotten anything. Two days before we were getting things in order and I had laid out my Santa bag, I asked Sarah, "Shouldn't this be filled with something?" The next day it was plump with packages visible from the top. What struck me as humorous was that I didn't have any first-day job jitters. I was totally comfortable with the task that lay ahead. Literally, I had made a list and was now checking it twice to be sure everything was in readiness.

As I sat in my favorite chair that night watching the news and a couple of our favorite TV shows, an advertisement came on the screen declaring that the Downtown Mall would be open the next day at 9:00AM sharp and that Santa would be there in person. I thought, *That's me.* I laughed a little, but then it hit me,

Did they say 9:00AM? I was told 10:00AM. I decided I'd rather be safe than sorry, which meant I should be there in plenty of time. *If I'm early, I'll just use the time in getting situated.*

I thought to myself, *Well, here I am embarking on a new career. Yes, it might be only a one-Christmas career, but I'm going to give it everything I've got.*

I was sure that by next year, I would be settled into a new job. What I was doing did seem like a lot of work for just one season. I thought, *Two months of preparation; one month of action. How's that for life in the fast lane?*

It was nice that my first party didn't start until December 1 because that meant I would have a whole week to smooth out the procedures at the mall and get accustomed to the work schedule. Sarah went to bed and told me not to stay up too late because she knew I had to get up a little earlier than usual in the morning. I checked my list thrice and went to bed. I had been thinking *Santa this* and *Santa that* for so long and so intensely that I was having Santa dreams. The fact that they weren't nightmares was a good sign to me.

I didn't seem to be hurried the next morning; I had my toast and drink and dressed almost ceremoniously. It almost felt as if I were getting ready to go to my sleigh and make my appointed rounds. I felt like something big was happening.

I was kind of disappointed when I had to climb into my Buick rather than into a beautiful sleigh to take me to the mall. I parked and drew several approving nods as I entered an employee door that would lead me down a corridor to the back entrance of the Santa setting. Mr. Burgess was there putting some last touches to the displays. He said, "My, you're early."

I told him of my TV experience and was told that they wanted to have me enter at ten o'clock with somewhat of a fanfare for the shoppers who had already arrived. I assured him I had plenty to do to keep me busy until then. They had provided me a small table and chairs inside of what looked from the outside like one of Santa's workshops. I would always enter the scene from that door when announced. It gave me a place to take a small break, if needed, to straighten myself up or just to have a minute to myself once in a while. I made sure that there was a large mirror available to allow me to check myself each time before going on stage.

About half past the hour, Haley arrived. I couldn't have been prouder of her. She had attached some little green velvet bows to the toes of her shoes; she had her hair in pigtails with a little gold bell attached at the very bottom of each of them; and, of course, she had "Freddy" her flute with her. We talked the routine over and decided that both of us would hand out candy canes. I told her she didn't have to bring every child up to me—she could bring a child just once in a while. "Just make sure things keep moving. In the meantime, you can talk to the children to find out what they want for Christmas. You can also help out a parent if necessary. Most of all, however, just be your elf—I mean *yourself*. And you can play your flute whenever you desire."

Of course I was sure that the more she played her flute, the better the Christmas atmosphere would be. I told her I would be getting up and down to move around often. "If you want to get off your feet for a while, feel free to just sit in Santa's chair. In fact, it'll be fun for the children to see Santa's little elf sitting in his big chair."

The chair was enormous in size. It seemed to make her happy that she wouldn't have just a minor role and could make decisions on her own.

At 9:45AM, an announcement came over the mall sound system that Santa would be arriving in fifteen minutes. We could hear a crowd gathering. Ten minutes later, they made another announcement. And for each minute of the last five minutes, they counted down from five to one and then, at 10:00AM, a voice over the sound system said, "Let's give a great big welcome to Santa Claus."

Haley and I opened the door and made our appearance. It was magical; there were hundreds of people gathered to see Santa. I headed one way around the arc and Haley went the other direction. Without any previous planning, we began greeting everyone, parents and children alike. The sound system blared out, "You better watch out, you better not cry, you better not pout I'm telling you why, Santa Claus is coming to town."

Some joined with the sound system and sang with the music. I stopped and led them when the song came to "So be good for goodness sake." I had to laugh to keep from crying because I was so moved by the number of people and the clapping and the dozens and dozens of smiling faces. *If only the world could capture this feeling*, I thought. *So many beautiful children. If I could only bring them together for one big group hug. This is what it's all about.*

I was thrilled as I looked through the crowd and saw my beautiful Sarah with Mabel and Ann clapping as enthusiastically as everyone else. Mabel and Ann were busy taking photos of everything that was happening. They seemed to be as happy with the reception as I was and found a personal pride with everything that was going on.

Pure joy showed in each face over and over again. If I had never been paid a penny, I would have already been compensated more than enough.

I gathered up several of the children and walked toward my throne. All the children followed, either drawn by the spirit of the moment or urged by a parent. It was one big mass of beautiful children. I had a large, round, soft red rug right in front of the chair, and I motioned for all the children to sit there. In turn, I sat on my throne and looked at my captive audience. My elf helped arrange them as she gathered them around me. She was perfect in comforting them as the need arose. I thought to myself, *She's good. No, she's **really good.***

Once they were settled, I placed a finger to my lips and motioned for silence. The music stopped playing, and we could have heard a pin drop. They waited in anticipation for me to do something magical. I drew it out just a little and then said, "Everyone who knows who I am, please shout out my name right now."

The response was unanimous, and shouts of "Santa" and "Santa Claus" were almost deafening as they filled the mall. I next motioned Haley to come over, and I asked the children as I pointed to her, "Who is this?"

They all knew, and they responded with "Elf," "Santa's elf," and "Santa's helper."

I told them that I had checked my reindeer the other night and that every one of them was ready to pull my sleigh. "Who knows the names of all my reindeer?"

Hands went up everywhere, I chose one very intelligent-looking young girl and said, "Could you come up and tell all the children the names of my reindeer."

There was no hesitation. She walked up, stood right next to me, and said, "There are actually nine reindeer: Dasher and Dancer, Prancer and Vixen. Vixen's my favorite. Comet, Cupid, Donner, and Blitzen. And then there's Rudolph."

I bent down and gave her a big hug. And then everyone clapped. I said, "I have a very important question to ask. Have you all been good children this year? Everybody who's been very nice this year raise your hand."

As hands shot up, Haley skittered down and acted as if to check each of them as she moved among them. She then said, "Every one of them, Santa."

I said, "Then we had better find out what you want for Christmas. Come up and tell Santa."

They all started up at once, and I didn't stop them. They were perfectly behaved. I placed one of them on my lap and two or three of them just leaned against my knees. One little fellow placed his elbow on my knee and rested his chin in the palm of his hand and looked up at me with wonderment in his eyes. He didn't want to miss a thing. I thought to myself, *Someone needs to get a picture of this.*

As I finished with one, another stepped up to take the next place. One little fellow even squiggled in the chair and sat beside to me. I let him stay for a while, and he proved to be a good helper. I think he would have been content to stay there the rest of the day.

Parents of course had to stay in the line except to take pictures. But children in Santa's playground have no boundaries. The picture taking started, as we hoped it would. The parents as well as some of the children used everything from large, complicated cameras to cell phones. The flashes just added to the glow that was everywhere.

Right on cue, Haley stepped into our workshop and came out with her flute. She played "Jolly Old Saint Nicholas," and the children were fully attentive. The minute she started, the mall sound system turned off, as if magic were in the air. We found out later that the person at the information counter, which was very close to us, controlled all sound. Obviously, we took precedence over everything else. Haley then said to the crowd, "If you know this song, sing along with me." She played "Rudolph the Red-Nosed Reindeer," and each one tried to outdo all others.

From Santa's perspective, when a song is known so universally, it requires admiration.

I picked up one little girl and placed her on my knee as she was singing. At that point, however, she wasn't quite ready for Santa just yet. So I joined in with the singing and added "Ho! Ho! Ho" in the right places. Children have minds of their own, thank goodness.

Throughout the day as I gathered the children wishes, I heard stories that made me laugh outright. I also listened to those that provoked a tear or two. I came to one conclusion—it's apparent at this young age that children can develop large caring and loving hearts. I was surprised at how many of their wishes were for other people. One little girl said, "Santa, will you please help my daddy get out of bed. He got hurt."

I could tell that several of the older children weren't quite sure whether I was the real Santa Claus. When I felt inspired to do so, I asked these children, "Do you believe in Santa?" In one case, a young boy said, "My older brother says that Daddy is really Santa. I wish he would let me go deliver presents around the world with him."

It was certain that Santa had to be very emotionally stable because the highs and lows came often and very unexpectedly. Children were so honest that they said what was in their hearts, and sometimes their hearts were breaking: "I wish my mom and dad loved each other." "We can't have Christmas this year because Daddy doesn't have a job." "My grandpa died, and I loved him. He always came over for Christmas."

In several instances, I thought, *Would that it were in my power to make everything right so these little hearts could be mended.* The most touching moments I had were with children in need. Sometimes all it took to solve their difficulties was to give assurance and a hug. *If only adults could be as resilient as children,* I thought.

Each night I found myself seeking another source of help. That is, each night as I prayed, I mentioned the children in need: "Tommy—please help make his dad better. Rosemary—please help her mother to get a job."

At one point when Sarah and I were talking about help from "another source," I merely said, "Well, I'm sure that Santa Claus believes in prayer."

Thank goodness for the many children who were filled with thousands of happy moments. There's no experience that equals a beautiful little girl looking into Santa's eyes and saying, "I love you, Santa." I know their love for a parent will never be equaled, but the love I felt from each child always felt genuine. I know that my love for them was authentic. I found myself saying, *Who could ask for a better profession than this?*

On one occasion at the end of the day, Martin told me that my elf and I were more than they could have ever hoped for. Haley and I staggered our breaks so one of us was always available for the kids, and we pretty well kept busy the whole day. Martin said that things would settle down into a routine after a couple of days and would even get more enjoyable with each passing day. I didn't know if I could take more joy than I was experiencing.

After telling Haley at the end of the first day how great she had done and being assured by her that she loved every minute of it, we hugged each other and headed home. I don't want to say arriving home was kind of a letdown, but after being the center of attention and being so busy for the previous eight hours, home seemed rather quiet. Of course, coming home to Sarah was never a letdown. After my first day at the mall, she said, "Come on. After your hard day's work, I have a proper Santa's dinner for you." She had made a wonderful beef stew with just the right balance of vegetables, and of course we had a loaf of her homemade French bread. We savored our dinner and didn't seem to be in a hurry to finish. I knew how tenderhearted Sarah was, and true to form, when I told her of some of the little children's difficulties, her tears flowed freely.

Thinking I should "liven" things up a little, I started telling Sarah about Haley. In going over each fun episode, I mentioned that Haley had played her role well. Sarah said, "Maybe it isn't a role. Maybe she's the real thing." At that, she laughed a little and trundled herself off to bed.

Later, as I took some time to reflect, I realized that Sarah's statement seemed to take on special meaning to me. I recalled numerous occasions from the past when we were driving down the street and saw people I called "characters" dressed in atypical style. I often asked Sarah, "If you were to cast that person in a movie, what role would you picture him in?" This became a game with us. We came up with characters such as "the villain," "the comic sidekick," "an innocent young woman," "the town idiot," and, on one occasion, "a zombie." Things reached the point that I tended to see everyone playing some role in life. Even with "normal-looking people," I found myself guessing at their roles—a parent, teacher, scientist, doctor, and so forth. This behavior led me to the question, *Is the role people play one they have chosen, or have circumstances in life forced them to play a role they would not have chosen?*

I assume that, in most cases, people choose a role because they want to play it. In a lot of cases, however, it's difficult to tell if people's lives are real of if they are just acting. Sarah has asked me on several occasions when we're "people watching," "Is he for real?"

I once heard a comment that illustrates what I mean. A friend who had attended a political rally the night before said to us, "The candidate took off his political hat and spoke frankly to us." I asked myself, *When he put on his political hat, did he not speak frankly?*

I recall the time when I was hired by Joe for my position in the company. He stated, "We'd like to ask you to act in the capacity of our public relations director."

I thought then, though I never said it, *Then you don't want me to be the real public relations director if I'm just to act the role for now?*

I still think about one of our employees who played the sick role more often than was necessary because it relieved him of the responsibilities of having to play other roles that were difficult for him to perform. The wonderful thing about life is that we can change our role whenever we want. We can't be forced to be the character if we choose not to play the role.

I came to the conclusion that we indeed can be "real" in doing the things we choose to do, even if it's only for a period of time or for certain occasions. Isn't this true for a woman who chooses to be a mother? How well she plays the role is what counts; that's what makes the role real. Anything that lessens her effectiveness as a mother diminishes whether she is a real mother or not. Therefore, if for a time Haley chooses to be an elf and plays the role well, she is for that moment or period a real elf.

Following this line of reasoning, I felt that for any occasion or any period of time I chose, I could be a real Santa.

8

Christmas Experiences

In talking about the role of Santa in a mall, when Martin had said, "It will eventually settle down to a routine." I don't know what he meant by that statement. The pace of being a Santa never settled down for me, and it never became routine. How could being a Santa be "normal"? A regular, everyday norm never set in. I learned from the past that people's days often promote tedious, monotonous, habitual routines. Such was never the case with my role as a Santa.

Every moment revealed another amazement, and I was often filled with wonderment more so than the children. I didn't want to miss a moment of this miracle. I was feeling sensations that had long been dormant—if they had ever existed. Don't get me wrong. I've always been a man who fully enjoys life; but now I was enjoying it on a higher level. I thought, *Most people might think that I have been **reduced** to being a Santa, but I'm enjoying life more than I ever have in the past."* I made a promise to myself, *From now on, I'll find happiness in everything I do; I'll make it my responsibility to either enjoy life or change it.*

Christmas has the wonderful ability to make everything and everyone better. Before I assumed the role of a Santa, I felt that patience and goodwill naturally can wear thin at Christmastime because of the crowds of people shopping in the mall, the delays in waiting to pay for purchases, and the dillydallying of people who seemed to be looking at window displays rather than paying attention to where they were going. Now, however, people seemed kinder and more tolerant and even helpful to each other.

In one instance, I watched as an older woman was heading to the parking lot with many more packages than she should be carrying. A young man went to her and, without any hesitation, gathered up several of her packages and escorted her out the door while his young wife or girlfriend waited patiently for his return. He returned soon thereafter and received an appreciative hug from a young lady who now obviously had a much greater admiration for him.

Such little kindnesses happened constantly. One day I saw a well-organized mother walking in the mall with her daughter in a stroller. She passed another mother who was holding a baby in one arm, leading a young son by the hand with the other arm, and pleading with her little daughter who was trailing behind to keep up. It didn't take the mother with the stroller much more than half a dozen steps before she stopped, looked back, thought for a moment, and then turned around and approached the mother with the three children. They talked for a couple of minutes. Then, the stroller lady lifted her daughter out of the stroller, turned around, and walked in the opposite direction, leaving her stroller with the mother and her three children.

After a few moments, the mother put her son in the front of the stroller, placed the baby behind him, and, after wiping the tears from her eyes, took her daughter by the hand and began pushing the stroller. I didn't hear the conversation that went on between these two mothers. All I know is that one mother had something to offer to help the other and saw fit to follow a prompting. I know that both felt better for what happened.

The Downtown Mall has around 130 stores. Each store plans its decorations for Christmas the whole year round. Oftentimes, the largest portion of a store's profits comes from Christmas sales. To walk the halls of a mall at Christmastime is like walking into a fairyland. It's always worth the time to visit a mall at Christmastime just to see humanity's offerings at their best.

It's especially amazing to look at all the different Christmas trees. I'm convinced that trees are some of God's greatest creations. The only way possible to improve them is to turn them into Christmas trees. There were literally hundreds of trees in the stores throughout the mall, and I became especially proud of the creativity of people who decorated the trees and was sure that even God loved all the improvements.

After school hours, and especially after school had been dismissed for the holidays, another reason young people loved Christmas, the youth would flock to the mall. The mall became their gathering place. Yes, they loved to shop, but they also loved to see each other and to be seen. Because youth take every occasion they can to draw attention to themselves, I was often used as their fall guy. I didn't mind. In fact, I began to enjoy it. They typically came by in groups. For some reason, being in a group seemed to give them an extra boost of confidence.

One day a group of teenage boys and girls came by. One of the boys yelled, "Hey Santa, what are you going to bring me this year?"

Without hesitation, I said, "Do you want another doll like you asked for last year?" Needless to say, he took a lot of ribbing from the group.

Sometimes a group of young people stopped and wanted to take a group picture with me. On one of these occasions, the group consisted of teenage girls. While the picture was being taken, one girl said, "Santa, I could surely use a cute boyfriend for Christmas." I told her that it shouldn't be difficult for a girl as cute as she was to find just the right guy.

At that point, a group of young boys who were about the same age as the girls approached us. They looked like good, clean-cut boys, so I called them over. I said, "Guys, Santa needs some help. This young lady wants a boyfriend for Christmas. I don't have one in my bag. Could one of you help me out?"

One of them looked at her and said, almost too enthusiastically, "I'll be glad to help you out," and then quickly added, "But only because it's you, Santa." They had quite a laugh, but all ended up walking off together. The girl yelled back, "Thanks, Santa."

Here's one more mall experience, and then I'll move on. Once in a while in a person's lifetime, an ideal situation just happens. Everything is right about it, and it provides a moment that could never be duplicated. Such an incident occurred a few days before Christmas, and its message will live on forever for those who were there.

Haley came out with Freddy her flute, sat on a large toadstool, and began playing "Silent Night." The sound system was turned off, and an unusual stillness permeated the mall. As if on cue, a little girl came out of the crowd and stood next to Haley. Sensing what was happening, Haley used what she had played thus far as an introduction and then began again from the first. "Silent night, holy night," came out of the girl's lips so pure it demanded attention. She and Freddy became one in proclaiming the carol's wonderful message.

Haley played while the young girl sang all the verses. The effect was as if an angel had been sent as a reminder of the purpose of Christmas and had brought her own heavenly accompaniment. Those gathered, including the children, stopped what they were doing and were spellbound while they tried to hear each word as the music expressed the story of a mother and child. I could feel the tears gathering, and I noticed that many of the adults and even some children were having the same reaction.

Those two, elf and child, will never meet to perform again, but those who heard the rendition will be closer to the true Christmas spirit than they could possibly be otherwise. Haley gave her new friend a hug and hurried into Santa's workshop. The child merely disappeared into the crowd. It took a while for Haley to gather herself before she came back out. When she finally returned, I just looked at her, nodded my head, and mouthed "Thank you!" We both understood the sacredness of the moment.

There were many such moments, all provoked by a time of year that promoted a feeling of caring. The thoughtfulness of those in the mall far outweighed the concerns of the commercial aspects of Christmas. The "Give me" nature of Christmas was far outweighed by the "Give to them" attitude. One day as literally thousands of shoppers were walking in the mall, I thought, *Every one of them is buying something for someone else. Yes, a few are probably looking for just the right clothes for the Christmas festivities they'll be attending, but most are looking for the perfect gift that will let other people know they are loved.* Thousands of acts of love can go a long way toward improving humanity.

The week in the mall went by all too fast; I wish Sarah could have been there to share personally the great experiences I was amassing. She seemed content to spend a few minutes with me as she listened to my reports of each day's activities and felt the spirit of what I was experiencing. When someone is as full of love as is my Sarah, that person will feel the whole spirit via the telling of each incident. I made sure that I never scrimped on any detail.

9

Starting the Christmas Parties

Taking on the role of Santa at the Downtown Mall was truly a unique experience; assuming the same role at company Christmas parties was different but just as unique. December 1 is the date the parties began.

I had looked forward to this time with great anticipation. With Company Christmas parties, I was now in the realm of the adult; however, I knew I liked to place each adult into the realm of a child.

I was very fortunate in being a Santa for company Christmas parties. It seemed that every company desperately wanted a good Santa for its party. Therefore, I had to spend very little time visiting companies to acquaint them with my services. From my mailings, I had received many replies, and I found that I needed to visit a company only once to secure the position and gather pertinent information for each party.

There are those who probably wonder how I could handle everything required of Santa. Even I wondered when I would totally wear out. Contrary to my worries, I was rejuvenated day after day by the experiences. I determined that I loved what I was doing and that love in itself is very invigorating. It then came to me as a revelation: *This is how Santa can keep going year after year and never seem to grow older. He gets so many recharges that he never wears out. Oh, and then there's the fact that Santa gets to rest for eleven months of the year.*

December 1 was a Saturday. We had a big snowstorm during the day that tailed off just in time for the party. The first storm of the year is always the best announcement that Christmas is not too far off. The snow enhanced the spirit of Christmas, and all at the party were ready to celebrate its coming. Most company Christmas parties are held in a wonderful restaurant, in a club setting, or in the company offices, and all have the most festive of feasts. All in attendance are dressed in their finest. In fact, the mundane business attire is replaced with clothes that say, "See, there's more to me than you see at the office every day; I do dress up good!"

My very first party was with the Wentworth Corporation. They responded to one of my mailers, and I made an appointment to go by and talk to a Mr. Evans. We met and talked for several minutes, and then he said, "I would like you to meet and talk to Mr. Wentworth himself. I think you and he have a lot in common." I assured him I didn't have to take Mr. Wentworth's time, as he was probably a very busy man. But Mr. Evans insisted.

Mr. Wentworth was not businesslike at all. In fact, he was very down to earth, and I was bettered for having met him. He asked me if I enjoyed playing Santa. When I answered, "Who's playing?" his laugh was as infectious as I wish mine could be. He said, "It looks like we have the right man, Tom."

He was very proud of his company and of all his employees. Without prompting, he started telling little stories on them that literally brought each employee to life. He seemed to know each of them intimately and was fond of them all equally. Needless to say, I was busy jotting down notes, which encouraged him all the more. It became evident that Mr. Evans was very proud of his boss and understood that if I was personally acquainted with him, I would be more effective in representing the company values.

At the party, after going around the room for hugs and handshakes and a rousing chorus of "Jingle Bells," I ended up at the top of the room. I said, "Mr. Wentworth, does a modeling agency do the hiring for your company? I've never seen so many beautiful girls."

After the laughs had died down, I added, "On the other hand, you must have hired the fellows for their talents." That brought out even more uproarious laughing.

I then asked for Joe Washburn to raise his hand. He was near the middle of the room. I said, "Joe, were you able to solve the problem with your wife's Christmas present last year? You remember what happened, don't you? I told the rest of them, "You see, his wife Mary told him that for Christmas last year she wanted something that would go from zero to a hundred in about six seconds. Joe instructed me to bring her a bathroom scale."

After the laughter had died down, I said, "Mr. Wentworth, it's easy to see that you have been a very good boss." This brought an arousing applause that was obviously very heartfelt. I imagined that this was all Mr. Wentworth needed to make his Christmas complete, so I asked him to come up and say a few words. Indeed, he said very few words, but what he said was very gracious: "I have only one thing that I want for this Christmas and that is for all of you to just stay the same. I'm very content with what you all offer to this company. Oh, and also, everyone have the merriest of Christmases." And then he sat down.

But he had said enough. After reacting to a few more Christmas requests, joking with them on a number of topics, and handing out a great Christmas ham and a beautiful, warm, woolen throw blanket to each employee, I ended my night at the Wentworth Corporation Christmas party.

At the next party that same night, I arrived a little early and was waiting in a back room. My host was a fellow in his thirties who sat and conversed with me. As usual, Christmas was the subject. He noted that he really loved the holiday seasons and that Christmas was always a big time for him. He was quick to let me know that he was not religious and that Christmas had no spiritual meaning for him. He said he had never believed in God. I've never known why people who have no religious beliefs think it's important to let others know their views. Do they want to convert others into believing that there's not a God, What would be their purpose in doing this. I think many times it's because of the shock value they believe it has on the listener. I merely said, "It's really not important whether you believe or not; it doesn't change the facts." I added that I *know* there is a God. He said, "There is no way you can really know; you probably just *believe* there's a God." I said, "Oh I know alright." He said, "I don't think you know I think you just believe?" I asked him, "Do you know that I believe, or believe I believe," and then I told him, "It's probably not overly important that you don't believe in God. What is important is that God believes in you."

The night went well. Ben McIntosh had recently been appointed as the new CEO for the corporation, and I asked if Ben was present. A hand was raised and several folks pointed at him. I had learned earlier that he was making large budget cuts and was tight with allocating monies. I said, "McIntosh—that's a Scottish name isn't it?"

To that question, he admitted proudly that he was Scottish, as all Scots do. I then asked if it was true that he had recently been made the company CEO. He nodded his head, and a few people clapped for him. I asked him if this meant a raise in income for him and got a hearty "Yes!" in response to my question.

I said, "Great, does this mean I might get Oreos and milk instead of vanilla wafers and water when I visit your home on Christmas Eve this year." The ensuing laughter was very appropriate.

We had a lot of fun with several employees, and everyone received a nice Christmas present and a company bonus. I went home satisfied with the day.

A couple of nights later at a party I said, "Everyone here think of what you want for Christmas, and when I point at you, just let everyone know what you want." After a minute or two, I started pointing. A young man yelled out, "A new set of golf clubs." I stopped the proceedings and said, "Who's responsible for employee relations? You need to watch his sick leave time closely this next year."

A young woman shouted out, "I want a big diamond ring."

I said, "What's your name?" She told me. I said, "Just a minute." I then went to my bag and pulled out a scroll that said *Nice* on it and feigned looking for her name. I motioned for more time, went back to the bag, and pulled out a black scroll that said *Naughty* on it. I said, "Oh, there you are. I can get you pretty close to a big diamond. How's your coal supply?"

As I was leaving this party, a fellow followed me into the foyer. He reached in his pocket, pulled out an envelope, and said, "My wife and I have been gathering our nickels and dimes throughout the year to help someone at Christmas, and we thought you might be able to use this better than we can." I thanked him, made sure that I had his name and address, and put the envelope in my bag.

That night I was going over the day's happenings with Sarah and remembered the envelope in the bag. I retrieved it, and together we opened it. Inside there were two $100 bills and two twenties. We were both somewhat shocked. Sarah said nothing; she just got up and went to the kitchen. I could hear her rattling around in the pantry. She came back with a large-size canning jar, took the money, and placed it in the jar. She stated her intention for the money by saying, "I'm sure we'll find someone who could really use this money." It never entered her mind that there may be many ways we could use the funds. Of course I agreed with her plan.

Often at the mall, someone came up to me, slipped a bill into my hand, and said, "Thank you." I always split this money with Haley, took the remainder home, and gave it to Sarah. I think she liked to watch the jar fill. I also had others at parties give me bonuses or feel an urge to help Santa out. Sometimes they would add a bonus when they paid for the night's activities. Anyway, the jar was filling nicely.

This brings up one of the most wonderful nights I spent at a party. Two things happened that were special. As I entered the building at the party and started preparing myself, a young man approached me and asked if I could help him propose to a young lady who was also a company employee. He handed me a ring box. We both checked it to view a rather wonderful ring. He left the ring with me, went in, and sat back at his table.

After a rousing welcome, I asked a few folks what they wanted for Christmas, and the tone was set. After several requests, I pointed at the young man and said, "What do you want most of all for Christmas?" He said, in a hesitant manner, "Well, I'd like to get me a wife."

The company had assigned seats at various tables, so he wasn't sitting next to his girlfriend. I said, "Why don't you come up here, and we'll see what we can do."

When we were together, I said, "Is there anyone here who will be his wife?"

Several hands shot up, and I said, "It looks like you have a choice."

I pointed at one of the ladies with her hand up and said, "Wait a minute. Isn't that your husband you're sitting next to? The laughter from the group was infectious.

Then, I pointed to the young man with whom I was in cahoots and said, "Do you see anyone you would like to marry?"

He said that he could see only one person and that her name was Jane. I asked if there was a Jane in the room, and a young lady held her hand up. I asked the young man if she was the right Jane, and he nodded that she was. I said, "Jane, do you want to come up?"

She feigned a no and then jumped up and almost ran to the stage. Once we were all together, I asked him, "Are you sure this is the right Jane?" He responded, "Yes!" And then I said to him, "Okay, what's your name?" He said, "Danny." I continued, "Okay, let me walk you through this. Danny, get down on one knee, face Jane, and take her by the hand."

Jane at this time was going crazy. I continued, "Look up into her eyes." He mimicked each direction. I then said, "Okay, repeat after me," and then said, "Jane." He repeated, "Jane." I then told him to ask her, "Will you marry me?"

He said it so sincerely and so full of emotion that every single girl in the house would have said yes. I then said, "Jane, now you repeat after me. 'Oh yes, Danny, thank you. I would love to be your wife.'"

There was no hesitation in her answer. I let out a big "Whew!" and wiped my brow. I reached into my pocket, pulled out the diamond ring, and said, "You had better give her this before she changes her mind."

I then said, "You may now kiss your fiancé."

The kisses reserved for such occasions never are the best, but theirs brought a standing ovation. The groups at the tables arranged for them to sit together the rest of the evening.

I said, "Did you see the size of that diamond? This company must be paying its employees well."

I contracted with this company to stay for two hours and had planned a program to fill that time. About midway through the agenda, the owner walked up and handed me a large bundle of envelopes. He gave a short speech and then added that because of the employees' devotion to the company, their bonuses were a little larger than last year's.

I thought to myself, *This will be fun. I'll just read the names on the envelopes and hand them out as they come up.*

I looked on the top envelope to call the first person, but the envelope didn't have a name on it. I got the nod to just hand them out. So I suggested that the employees at each table should come up to get their bonuses as I pointed to their table. In the back of my mind, I initially wondered how I would know which envelope to give to those who had worked for a number of years and therefore deserved a larger bonus. The envelopes were all handed out, and there was one left over. I said, "Have we forgotten someone?"

The owner said, "That one's yours, Santa. After all, you're a company employee as of today, and you also deserve a bonus."

I assured him I didn't deserve a bonus because I had worked only one night in the whole year. He and every employee there insisted that I keep the bonus. I guess they were all used to the company bonus policy.

I found out later that the policy of the company was that it didn't matter how long an employee had worked for the company. This would be the only company bonus an employee would get, and the fact that one employee hadn't work as long as others didn't mean that employee's needs were less. All had needs, so all bonuses would be equal. People who had longevity were already rewarded with larger salaries to satisfy their worth to the company.

I put my envelope in the bag and went home to Sarah. We opened the envelope together and were stunned at the amount: $1,000. It was in the form of a cashier's check made payable to the bearer. Sarah, a little giddy, placed it in the jar. She said she would cash it tomorrow. When I got home the next night, our jar had an additional fifty $20 bills added to it.

After a short discussion, we decided to keep, as much as we could, a list of all such gifts. It was our intention to write and let all donors share in the joy of giving and to let them know how their funds were used. We would just make an end of the year donor's newsletter and add each story, without names of course, as the Christmas year progressed. Each donor would know that they played a part in each story.

After Sarah had retired, I replayed the day in my mind. I surely didn't deserve such a generous bonus. *What could they be thinking?*

The word *deserve* to me meant that I had done something to merit such a reward. Maybe it had nothing to do with what I ought to have done as much as what I ought to be. If I'm told through a bonus that I am an equal with all other employees, I will want to make myself worthy of the perception. If employees understand that they're valued, they will more likely become valuable.

The monies we were collecting were becoming a significant amount, and that increased the responsibility I felt about their disposal. When the money was given, I was impressed that

I was never once told I would be held accountable for its use. In my mind, that of course increased my degree of accountability. I reasoned with myself that for every dollar given, there were thousands of needs existing. I wanted to make each dollar achieve its maximum worth.

I then reasoned that Santa needed another list. I decided to make that list, which was not a list of the needy but a list of anything that came to my mind that would give me information and knowledge of how to discern worthy recipients. The list went something like this:

Everyone needs help; it's my duty to find what it is that's required:

1. Who are the needy?

After much thought and a little research, I came to the conclusion that there is not a person living who doesn't have some kind of a need. Anyone I meet may be a prospect. A majority of needs could be handled with little cash outlay, or maybe no cash would be needed. It doesn't matter how small a need is. If a person can't meet the need's requirement, it is still a need, they were in need of a rescuer.

2. How can you truly tell if someone deserves help?

I recalled an old Swedish proverb my dad taught me: "Help me when I least deserve it because that's when I most need it." Once again, I realized that we couldn't rule out anyone's needs. I determined that I would rather err on the side of generosity.

3. How big or how small should the gifts be?

Of course, this doesn't mean in size. It asks whether I should use less money per person and thus give to many more or whether I should I spend it all on one situation if the need demands it. Once again, it doesn't matter if it is a big need and a small need, if a person can't handle it themselves, they need help.

4. How do I give without embarrassing the recipient?

Sometimes, just giving a gift to someone in need is a way of telling that person that he or she is among the less fortunate—a state that individuals may not believe they have reached. The manner of giving is sometimes as important as the gift given.

5. How do I find someone in need?

What sources are available that would lead me to those in need? I could visit local churches, Chambers of Commerce, hospitals, local news bureaus, etc. I had already concluded that because the funds came from local sources, they should be distributed within the community.

I clearly discerned that this part of being a Santa as a career could end up being the most difficult. It probably required the qualifications for which I was the least trained. This thought process caused a kind of remorse I didn't expect. Throughout my life, to that point, I probably had not been aware of the needs of others as much as I should have been. I asked myself sadly, *Have I not had enough love for others to be aware of their concerns?"* My answer gave me little relief: *There's no one I really dislike. I have a fondness for all people, but do I love them to the point that I care for them?*

How many individuals have I really helped? Is there a degree of worry or anxiety when I find others are having problems? *There should be*, I reasoned. *Do I even know when they're having difficulties in life?*

I consoled myself with the thought, *I have so little to give.*

But this approach gave me no peace as I thought, *That's my fault. Any person can increase their capacity to provide in many ways what people require for a happy existence.*

This reasoning, of course, provided the answer I was looking for: *Where happiness is missing, there I should be. The greatest happiness can be delivered only when the source of unhappiness is known.*

Finding a person with a need simply equates to finding an unhappy person. This would require me to be a lot more aware and to be caring of others' concerns. In other words, I would have to learn how to love. A line from one of my favorite Christmas movies, *The Grinch Who Stole Christmas*, came to mind: "Unless someone like you cares a whole lot, nothing is going to get better. It's not."

I became need oriented. For example, the next morning I had my drink and toast as usual, but my paper-reading habits changed considerably. Instead of reading just the news and sports, I lingered over items reporting setbacks or problems people were having. One article, for some reason, brought a myriad of thoughts to my mind. It concerned a wealthy man in our community who had just donated a new wing to a local hospital. I laughed a little at myself when I thought, *That's a worthy cause; maybe Sarah and I could donate Santa's funds to help out.*

I could see the result—a toilet in the restroom with a plaque on it that read, *This was donated by Santa Claus.* That would probably be all my funds could purchase. But it wouldn't be very practical.

And what about the donor responsible for the new wing at the hospital? I reasoned. *Is he in need of a proper thank you from a grateful community? Will he be unhappy if he isn't recognized? Will he be happier if he is given proper recognition?*

I was sure the wing would be named after him. But did he *know* that some little folks in the community really appreciated him? If nothing else, that knowledge would increase his happiness. *Maybe I should also look for ways to make the happy even happier.* I wrote his name on the pad for consideration: *James T. Harrington.*

10

Token of Appreciation

My regular Santa efforts took a new direction. I started listening to and watching everyone for any hint of unhappiness. I found that unhappiness is obvious in many ways and can easily be detected. Any despondency or gloom, such as exhibited by a little melancholy, discontentment, or even a lack of smiling, is a symptom indicating a degree of unhappiness. I found it easy to identify unhappiness in people and wondered why I hadn't been doing it all my life.

The next day in the mall, a young boy found his way onto my lap. I asked his name and where he lived, and then we started talking. He told me that his dad was in "Afgan," as he called it. I asked him if his dad would be home for Christmas and was told "No." I found out that he had a sister younger than he was. I then assured him that he could have a wonderful Christmas with his mother and sister. He told me that their car had broken down, that his mother had to put a new engine in it, and that she had said to him and his sister, "Well, there went all the Christmas money." The gloominess in his voice gave away his unhappiness.

We finally got around to talking about what he wanted for Christmas, and he said he would like to have a Lego Bat Cave. His sister wasn't there, but he knew what she wanted, a Talking Doll Ellen. I called Haley over and privately told her to run to the toy store, which was just across the hall, talk to Mr. Henley the manager, and tell him I want a Lego Bat Cave and a Talking Doll Ellen. "Have him wrap them up and tell him I'll be right over to pay for them. Run as fast as you can."

She smiled and confirmed that she knew her mission. I took the boy by the hand and followed him as he led me to his mother. He said, "Mom, this is Santa." She gave me a guarded smile. I asked her if she were going to be in the mall for a while. When I got an affirmative answer, I made her promise that she would come back in half an hour. I then told her son to make sure that she did, and he promised me they would return.

Not much later, Haley came back smiling all over. I don't know how she does it, but her whole being seems to smile. She had a large store bag with two beautifully wrapped presents in it. I asked if she could watch things while I ran over and paid the bill. In her elfish way she said, "It won't be necessary. Mr. Henley told me to tell you that this one is on the house. He said you would know what he means."

I thought, *Elf number four.*

It wasn't too much later that mother and son returned, promptly right on the half hour. I told them I had sent my elf to get their Christmas presents early and handed them the bag. I made them promise they would not open the presents until Christmas morning. I whispered to the mother and told her what was in the package. Any semblance of unhappiness had left both of their faces, and, for the moment, they were happy. A thought came to me, *Unhappy times are merely those periods between happy times; all I have to do is find ways to reduce the occurrence of unhappiness, or increase the frequency of happiness.*

That evening, I was telling Sarah about the incidents of the day. She was delighted and said, "How can we ever thank Mr. Henley? You've certainly gained another elf, and he should be rewarded."

I stored that one in my head and also made a note for future use: *How do I reward my elves for what they've done?* I said to Sarah, "That reminds me of Mr. Harrington." And then I shared the story of James Harrington with her, including especially his generous donation to the hospital and community. I asked her what gift would let a man like this know he is appreciated. She said, "I think it's a wonderful idea, Robert. He probably needs love as much as anyone. There must be some little token we could give him."

The force of her words was the birth of an idea. Maybe each year at Christmastime a person could be singled out and honored for making the community a happier place. This choice would be solely at the discretion of Santa Claus, as the reward must come from him. A coin could be forged with the inscription, *Token of Appreciation*, and could be mounted along with a letter stating the reason for the choice. I remembered the trophy shop in the mall and the way they displayed beautiful award medallions for the public to see. Maybe they could make me the perfect coin—or "token" in the words of Sarah.

Once again the call went out to Barb Barwick. I found that she had secured employment, but it wasn't to start until the first of the year. Without my asking, she said, "I'm available to help; what's needed?"

I told her of my project, and she thought it was brilliant. I told her it was my wife's idea. She said, "Then you'll want a design for the coin, a layout for an award notification, and a proper way of presenting the award."

I reminded her of the time restrictions and was told not to worry. That same afternoon, I received a call on my Santa cell. It was Barbara asking when we could meet. I told her I had two parties that night and wouldn't be home till late. I explained that I had to leave at 9:30 in the morning to get to the mall on time.

And then I said, "Other than those conflicts, I can fit you in at any time." She laughed and asked if I could spare a minute if she were to come to the mall. I told her to come at her convenience, which turned out to be just an hour later.

We retired to Santa's office while Haley watched the store, so to speak. Barb had found a wonderful coin template and was able to insert the proper words. In the center of the front of the coin was an impression of Santa's head. Above the head, arched in bold letters, were the words *Token of Appreciation*. At the bottom was the word *Christmas* followed by the year. On the flip side was a beautiful reindeer in full stride. Above that, instead of *United States of America*, the city name was printed. At the bottom where the coin value is normally printed, it read *100 Blessings*. It was absolutely perfect. The presentation package was simple; it was merely a frame with a velvet coin indent at the top to hold the coin in place. Below that was space to enter a well-worded letter stating the reason the award was given. Barb suggested a salutation and font for the lettering. The letter would be signed at the bottom in person, with red ink, by Santa Claus. She said I would have to write the salutation and the letter myself.

I told her I had to get back to "my children." I was concerned whether she was getting along okay without a paycheck and was told that she had planned well for such a setback. I then gave her a Santa hug and thanked her profusely. *I've certainly chosen my elves properly*, I said to myself. *But I have to come up with some way of rewarding them.*

Other opportunities to help started presenting themselves almost daily. There were so many of them, now that I was being more observant, that I started fretting about having enough funds, even though they were still coming in generously. My biggest worry was figuring out how I was going to get everything done—the shopping and wrapping, obviously, but mainly the deliveries. How was I going to get these offerings to everyone on

Christmas Eve? *Well*, I thought, *If Santa can visit the whole world in one night, I ought to be able to cover my one city. I'm certainly glad I asked for the day and night off. Christmas Eve is going to be very busy.*

I ran over to the trophy store and showed them the layout for the coin and the presentation. I wanted the coin to be about the circular size of a large orange in a gold color that would never lose its luster. He said they did not have a way of making the coin, but he knew of a company that did and would be happy to follow through for me. I was assured that the presentation frame could be done very nicely. I gave him the go-ahead and let him know that I had only until December 24 to have the project completed.

As I was getting ready to leave the mall that night, I stopped off at the Chocolate Factory, a store in the mall that carried chocolates to die for. I bought several half-pound boxes of chocolates. I was scheduled for only one party that night, and it was at a later hour. I had an hour and a half to stop by the Elderly Care Center. This was an assisted living center, and if my timing was just right, I could be there right at their dinnertime when they were all together.

The receptionist was thrilled to see me and led me right to their cafeteria. I half skipped in with a "Merry Christmas" to everyone. There were many reasons for them to be there—lots of medical and mental issues—but most were merely incapacitated enough that professional help was needed. None of them were so disabled that they could not produce large smiles on their faces when they saw Santa. They all knew Santa, and apparently they all loved chocolates. For just a few moments in lives otherwise lacking in incentive, they were able to feel a degree of joy. People this age know their candy well and are most appreciative of high-quality chocolates.

One lady was sitting by herself and seemed more sullen than the others—obviously a sign of unhappiness. I made her the object of my attention. I walked over to her and asked, "What do you want for Christmas, little girl?"

I didn't know if that was the right thing or the wrong thing to say because tears started flowing down her cheeks. When she started talking, I could tell she had most of her faculties working well. She said, "If only you were the real Santa and could bring me what I really want for Christmas."

I asked what that was, and she replied, "Oh, never mind. That's just life, isn't it?"

I asked her to tell me her name, and she proudly said, "Rosemary Gough." I said, "Rosemary, I'm the *real* Santa Claus." That drew a little chuckle out of her.

I stopped at the receptionist desk on the way out and gave the receptionist my last box of chocolates. I asked her about Rosemary. The receptionist said, "She's one of our finest patients. She's so kind and thoughtful, but she's not given very long to live. She has one daughter in town who almost lives at the center to take care of her mother, and then she has two other children who live out of town."

The receptionist's insight spoke well of her love for the people in the center. I was told that Rosemary's only wish was that she could spend Christmas with her children. It didn't seem like too big of a request, and I asked why the children couldn't come and visit her. The receptionist told me they were trying to make it happen, but her two children didn't have the money to make the trip. It seemed that with their mother's medical bills and the cost of the care center, which they all shared equally, they had nothing left and would probably not even have much of a Christmas themselves because of the added costs.

I wrote down the address and phone number of the daughter in town and decided that tomorrow I would see what could be done to help. I called the daughter at nine o'clock the next morning and told her, "This is Santa."

She replied, "Of course it is."

I then detailed for her my visit with her mother the previous night and asked, "Would you like the whole family to come so they could be with you and their mother for Christmas?"

She told me all the implications. They of course couldn't come without their spouses. One of them has a daughter. And even by pooling all their money, there just wasn't enough. But yes, they wanted to come ever so much. "It would be the best thing that has ever happened for our mother, and then she added with an almost certain confirmation that this might be her mother's last Christmas."

When I asked if they had looked into the flight cost, she had an immediate answer. For the five of them, the round-trip fares would be just short of $1,500. I told her to call without delay and tell the families to start packing. She couldn't talk for a while; all I heard over the phone was very noticeable sobbing. She gained control of herself and stated that things like this just don't happen to her. I told her I would have a check for her tomorrow. I planned on adding a little more for food and celebration.

One of the dreams of my heart would have been to have the opportunity to be there when her daughter brought her mother home for a reunion with the entire family. I gave her daughter one stipulation that she had to do for me. She had to say to her mother at the right time, "Santa told me to tell you that he is real." And then I added, "She'll know what you mean."

When I told Sarah the night before what I was going to try to do, she began tearing up a little and said, "Oh, Robert, if there's not enough in the jar, let's add a little ourselves." This was not required, but it reminded me of my love for my wife's willingness to share. I made a note to leave early the next morning to drop off a check for the airfare.

The daughter must have seen me coming up the walk, as she ran out and met me. Needless to say, Santa received another hug of love. There are a lot of hugs given in life, but none are as impressive as those filled with deep emotion.

The whole Santa experience kept my wife and me on what I called a "Christmas rollercoaster with great highs as well as great lows." We had a difficult time coping with story after story of people who were caught up in difficulties that were usually not of their own making. In fact, we were all but literally broken-hearted when we heard some of the stories.

During the stages of my being a Santa, I found that life can place people in dilemmas they have no way of solving without help. I discovered that every person at one time or another can use a dose of help—a helping hand—just to get over a hump in life. Sometimes that dose of help requires no more than a caring individual who will take the time to rally around someone who is having a difficult time.

The need for a dose of help doesn't affect only the poor and needy; anyone can be subject to a loss or be hindered in life from a hundred causes. Life is so full of decisions and adversities that few people are exempt. The thing that makes it possible to live with heartbreak is the kindness shown by those who help. Wherever a problem is present, a good deed is needed. Whenever people face adversity there should be someone to help them. Every person has unique abilities, although they can't help everyone they should be able to help some. This is probably the best reason to increase ones capabilities, the more capable you are the more services you can render.

I was learning that by being Santa, I offered myself to others as someone with whom they could share their needs. It seemed like all the people I met knew one thing for sure: Santa loves them. In fact, Santa represents the good in all people, and all people deep down in their souls want to be good.

11

Christmas gets Serious

Hundreds of little Santa-related needs kept presenting themselves. I had the means of helping with many of these needs, but once in a while those little incidents that I mentioned earlier would just pop up to solve a problem far better than I ever could have; they can happen in the most peculiar ways.

For example, our city supports an NBA basketball team. Frankly, that team is what keeps me reading the sports page every morning. I really love my basketball. However, I knew that one of my little sacrifices for being a Santa was that I'd have to wait until after Christmas to start watching the games again. We have one of the premier point guards in the nation on our team. The only thing he was better at than playing basketball was being a good human being. Our whole town loved him.

It wasn't odd, then, that Santa got many requests from the kids for basketball jerseys with this player's number on them, and NBA basketballs. On one occasion when I asked a young man what he wanted for Christmas, he told me he wanted tickets to go to one of the ballgames. He had never been to a professional basketball game. He told me that his dad had said, "The tickets are just too costly; we have to watch every penny I bring home. Maybe someday and someway we'll be able to go."

I couldn't blame the father. The food on the table and clothing were far more important to his family than the excitement of a basketball game. In fact, I deemed him a great father. The lad was old enough to know his own address and telephone number, so I collected them from him. Of course I was going to see that he and his dad would get to go to a game.

The very next day, coincidence again, as I sat on my throne, I looked down the line of children. Coming up in the line was our famous point guard with his little daughter. I thought, *Why not? He's a father like anyone else.*

I don't know if I hurried the line a little intentionally, but soon he was standing in front of me with his daughter. I said "Merry Christmas" and treated them as I did every other parent and child. I found out his daughter's wishes and then asked if *he* had any wishes as I joked a little and said, "Like a win against the Lakers?" He said that would be nice.

I said, "I have to tell you something. Thanks for being the person you are."

He replied, "Someday I may be as good as Santa."

We both laughed. He then said, "I have a question. What does Santa get for Christmas?"

I hadn't been asked that before, but it was a valid question. I told him that all Santa wants for Christmas is a world full of happy people. And then the little boy from the day before came to mind. I pointed out to our point guard that maybe he could help me with something special. I rehearsed the story to him. He asked if I had a way of getting hold of the boy. I reached into my pocket, found the piece of paper with the boy's address and phone number on it, and handed the paper to him. He said, "I'll handle it from here. I'm all over it. Merry Christmas." And then he and his daughter left.

I thought to myself, *He's going to rack up one more assist. I wonder how many assists he's had that aren't in the stat books.* Can you imagine having one of the finest NBA point guards as one of your elves?

Two days later, the boy and his father showed up at the mall to thank me. This fine, young ballplayer had driven to their home that day and had given them seats in the executive suite for the whole family to watch a game that would be played the day after Christmas. They would have a food buffet and everything to enjoy. And then he gave them a real NBA basketball signed by all the team members. I thought, *Santa couldn't have done it as well.*

I went into a party that night feeling just a little intimidated. This was one of the largest law firms in the city. I usually joked a little at each party about the kind of business the company did. I didn't know if lawyers liked lawyer jokes, so I asked the fellow who hired me if I could tell a few lawyer jokes. He said that there was one lawyer in the firm who collected lawyer jokes because he was going to publish a book with all of them included. I was then told that the firm's attorneys loved lawyer jokes.

I learned from this occasion that those with serious occupations can find great relief in not taking themselves too seriously all the time. I don't know if it is just being so straight-laced while studying cases, arguing in court, or just getting away from mammoth responsibilities, but I found that the members of this group, who dealt with the serious side of life, had a true fix on life's importance and knew it must be celebrated. What I thought was going to be a stodgy group became one of the most enjoyable, fun-loving bunches I had yet visited.

They were a rowdy bunch. After my usual grand entrance and after I finally had their attention, I admitted that I just didn't know what lawyers wanted for Christmas. I said, "Could you help me out here a little?"

I got everything from "the day off" to "a large, wealthy client." I said, "It must really be cold out tonight. When I arrived, I saw several lawyers with their hands in their own pockets." The ensuing laughter prompted other lawyer jokes. *Where's this going?* I asked myself.

Eventually, I asked if there happened to be a judge in the crowd. Two men raised their hands. I threw one a Christmas package and told him to open it and tell us about his Christmas present. After opening the package and examining its contents, he said, "It's a pair of cufflinks. This one has the word 'Guilty' on it, and the other one has the words 'Not guilty' on it. What am I supposed to do with them?"

I replied, "The next time you have to render a tough judgment, just look at one of your cufflinks. That'll make it easier for you to decide between guilty and not guilty."

I had been given the name of one attorney who had recently negotiated a large settlement. I said to the group, "Did you know that Santa needs a lawyer once in a while? In fact, I need a good lawyer right now. Is Jerry Hansen here?"

He stood right up. I said to him, "I was told you're a good lawyer and might be able to help me with a friend who's in trouble."

He warily said, "I can try." Spoken like a true lawyer.

I said, "He was arrested for Christmas shopping early. Is that a problem?"

He said, "I can't see any problem getting him off. There's no law against Christmas shopping early. Why did they even charge him?"

I said, "Well, you see, he went into the store at four in the morning, but it didn't open until ten." As usual, the laughter was very loud.

We handed out a few more little gifts, sang a couple of carols, had the senior partner say a few words, and then, in closing, I said, "How many of you think Santa is real?"

Hands went up all over the room. I then said, "I'll leave you with a little riddle. You work it out. Three people—a kind lawyer, an honest politician, and Santa Claus—walked into a store where all three saw a $20 bill on the floor. Which one picked it up?"

I gave them some time to think about it, and it wasn't long before the room echoed with the groans of those who had figured it out.

For some reason, I felt prompted to leave this group on a serious note. Standing next to a large candle, I said, "Santa wants to thank you seriously for sorting out people's problems, and even though you're compensated, it's a true act of kindness. Every community needs men and women who have prepared themselves to represent those who don't have the proper ability to represent themselves when facing problems. You're like this candle. It's lovely at Christmastime; it brings a little light into the world; it doesn't make a whole lot of noise; and it just sits back and glows. But in order to give a little light to the world, it slowly gives itself away."

I waved, wished them all "Merry Christmas," and left slowly. As I sat in my car, I thought, *That's probably what Santa would have done in this situation.*

I arrived home a little later than usual. Sarah was already prepared for bed, so I told her to go to sleep without me. "I'll catch you up on everything in the morning."

I was in a pensive mood after my meeting with the attorneys. Christmas had taken a serious turn, and I was glad for the time to reflect on it. I thought, deep down, *There's probably more to Santa than meets the eye. Under his joyful exterior, there's probably a man with a very heavy heart. Even I'm getting to the point that it's difficult to observe any degree of unhappiness in people. But how can you not get a little sorrowful when the cares of the world become your problem?*

The answer was so evident that I wondered why I had the concern or the uneasiness in the first place. Mentally, I summed up everything: *Santa's whole purpose, his whole reason for existing, is to bring joy to the world. If even one degree of unhappiness is removed, the world is a happier place. Santa's whole work is to find and help unhappy people. The more problems **he** can solve, the happier **he** is. Does anyone really think that there's a problem that can't be lessened? No problem can withstand the bombardment of love. With that revelation in mind, I'm in a beautiful situation; I can make a difference in many lives. And I'm certainly happier than I've ever been in my life.*

I reminded myself that I needed to get Mr. Harrington's token-of-appreciation certificate composed and over to the trophy shop first thing in the morning. After many attempts to create a message that would let our gracious donor know his contribution to the city had not gone unnoticed and was appreciated, I came up with the following:

This Token of Appreciation is awarded to Mr. James T. Harrington by Santa Claus. This annual award is presented to one person in the city at Christmastime to let this person know that his or her gift to society has not gone unnoticed. Yours is a gift of wellness to thousands of future patients for many years to come, and exemplifies the true spirit of Christmas. May you feel the joy and the blessings of all people as they are blessed and healed because of your gift of health and love.

Santa Claus

I next turned my thinking to a gift I could give to each of my elves. Chocolate or fruit or anything similar just didn't sound right because they, my elves, were so very special. I came up with the idea of presenting them with a plaque making them honorary Santa's elves. I wanted to turn this one over to Barb but thought it would be tacky having her design her own present. In the end, I found a wonderful picture of an elf leaning through a holy wreath with a big red bow on it. I would merely insert each elf's picture professionally on the elf's face and have the plaque read as follows:

HONORARY SANTA'S ELF

This is to certify that ---name--- has been given the status of Honorary Santa's Elf.

This honor is bestowed because of the many unselfish moments and kind acts while in Santa's service. The bearer of this certificate is entitled to be viewed as a real Santa's Elf.

Santa's elves positively affect people's lives because of services they have rendered.

They are the best examples of the true spirit of Christmas.

Santa Claus

I made plans to have this made into nice plaques by the trophy store and personally have Santa present the plaques to my elves on Christmas Eve.

12

Santa's Progress

One of my big problems with the Christmas season is that it is just not long enough. They could start it after Halloween for all I care. It was certain that this year's season would seem the shortest I ever spent. The days flew by, and it wasn't long until I was looking at only one week left—just seven more shopping days until Christmas. I was still having fun and hadn't yet reached the top of my learning curve on how to be Santa.

For instance, I've learned to be cautious about drawing conclusions based on initial perceptions. One day a young lad sat on my knee. I decided to have some fun with him because he had a trace of egg yolk on the side of his face. I asked him if he had been a good little boy, and he answered, "Of course." I wanted to impress on him the fact that Santa always knows everything about little boys and girls, so I told him that I even knew what he had eaten for breakfast that morning. When he asked, "What?" I told him, "Eggs." He thought for a moment and said, "No! I had eggs yesterday morning. I had Cheerios this morning."

So much for that lesson on perceptions, I muttered to myself. *And so much for my thinking that mothers always wash their kids' faces.*

On another occasion, a thirty-three-year-old science major masquerading in a nine-year-old girl's body sat on my knee, and when I asked her what she wanted for Christmas, she said, "Really nothing. But I do have a lot of questions I would like answered."

Not knowing what I was up against, I told her very confidently to ask her questions. I'm not clever enough to remember everything exactly, but her first questions went something like this: "How many miles an hour does your sleigh go, and do you have to allow time for storms? For example, how long does it take you to fly from the United States to Great Britain, and what route do you follow each year?"

I said to myself, *How can I answer such questions—especially when I've never made such trips?*

However, I recovered my composure quickly when pure inspiration hit me. I just gave a little laugh to indicate the easiness of the answer and said, "You know, of course, that there's no speedometer on a sleigh. Sometimes I have to slow time down a bit to make it everywhere in one night."

She picked right up on that one, making me realize that I'd have to be more careful with my answers. She said, "But how do you slow time down?"

I had one of those moments of almost pure genius when I said, "Have you ever waited for something that you really wanted, like Christmas morning to get here or the Thanksgiving turkey to get done, and time moves so slowly that you thought Christmas would never get here or that the Thanksgiving turkey would never be ready to eat?"

"Yes," she said.

I then told her that in such instances, someone had just slowed the time down. "That's what happens to me on Christmas Eve." To her, this seemed logical, and she was satisfied.

She next asked me if there was a Mrs. Santa Claus, and I told her, "Yes, and she's wonderful!"

She then asked, "How many children do you have?"

At that point, I knew I was in over my head, so I explained that I needed to move on to the next child in the line. As she was getting down, she asked, "Are you rich?"

I answered, "Of course not. That's why I'm sometimes called St. Nickel Less." That got me a good laugh and a good way to end.

I was starting to plan my last few days, especially Christmas Eve. I knew I would be working on a time schedule, and I didn't want to forget anything. I started another list:

1. Elf present delivery, Mable, Ann, Alex, Barbara, Mr. Henley, basketball player.

2. Get something for Haley

3. Deliver Harrington token

I stopped at that point right in the middle of making the list and thought, *I've got to check on Sarah's gift. I've got a perfect wife, so I must get her a perfect gift. Sarah has always liked gifts that are meaningful. This will require some deep thinking. But this year, the gift I select has to be even more meaningful than ever. After all, I am Santa this year.*

I added her name to the list. I also added the name of a company that never has Christmas parties.

And then, in thinking of James Harrington, I said to myself, *Because his gift will be to the community, the whole community should be made aware of his award. The best way for this to be accomplished would probably be by TV and newspaper coverage. The news media are always looking for a special-interest story around Christmas time, they just might like this one. I'll call the local media outlets in the morning and tell them of the event.*

The next morning I first made a call to James Harrington's home. I was hoping I would get to talk to him directly and not to a house servant or secretary. His name was listed in the local directory, and I could tell it was the right number and address because of the location. I dialed the number, and someone picked up the phone on the first ring. True to the nature of a giving person, he had not secluded himself. It was Mr. Harrington himself who answered.

I identified myself as Santa Claus and asked him if it was possible to pay him and his family a visit on Christmas Eve. He said, "I don't know why not. You've been coming every year for some time now."

His laugh gave good clues about his kindness. He asked the time of my visit, and I told him at 4:00PM. He hesitated a little and asked if I might make it at 5:00PM instead. He told me that by then, all his family and grandkids would be there. He didn't want to put me out but said he would love it if his grandchildren could have a visit with Santa. I thought this a marvelous idea and agreed on the time. I never mentioned the award because I wanted to keep it a surprise.

I hurried and called Channel 4 News and was directed to one of their newscasters. I introduced myself as Santa and explained the award presentation and the nature of the Token of Appreciation. They thought it would be a great human-interest story, especially because James Harrington was a very prominent figure in the community. They assured me they would have a team there to cover the occasion. They kept me on the line long enough to get all the important information needed to build a good story. I was quite pleased and impressed with their reception.

I next called the local newspaper and got the same enthusiasm. They turned me over to one of their writers, and I was a little surprised that they wanted so much information on me. I never told them my real name or address because I thought any mention of either would detract from the real story, which was James Harrington. "This story isn't about Santa," I said.

13

The Hospital Visit

I had only one night the entire Christmas season that I didn't have at least one party scheduled—December 18. I could have scheduled the night several times but wanted to keep it clear so I could make a special trip to the Children's Hospital. I called them earlier to see if it would be all right for Santa to make a visit. They had received many donated gifts to be distributed to the children but had not engaged a Santa. They told me they had called a couple of fellows they knew but were unsuccessful because both men were too busy this time of year. I told them to count on me for the whole night and received a very grateful thanks.

We laid out a few ground rules so the visit could be as effective as possible. I asked if I could have a nurse go with me into each room so I wouldn't cause any problems with medical procedures. "And can somebody make certain I have the right present to give to each child. I don't want a little girl getting a little boy's present or vice versa."

I told them I would arrive right at 7:00PM and could stay until every child was visited. I asked them if they could let all the children know I would be coming. "Anticipation is the best part of a Santa's visit, so please tell them I'll be bringing presents." Then a thought came to me and I asked, "How many presents are there for each child?" I was told they had enough to give them three each so far. I told them that Santa wanted to give each child only one present, and I explained that I thought it important for the nurses or others to distribute the rest of the presents. "This will allow them to get to know each other and help the children bond closer to hospital personnel." I thought to myself, "Love is the best healer."

As for me, I found myself looking forward to the hospital visit all season long. I thought to myself, *What is it that these children need most in life?* The answer came to me quickly and was simple: *Hope. This, of course, must be followed with a large dose of love.* I felt that all I had to do was awaken their souls to awaken their hope. I had to let them know that hope is the feeling, and that the feeling they were having isn't permanent. The hope I could instill in them for tomorrow would wipe away the pain they felt in their lives today.

I knew that any number of reasons created the necessity for placing the children in the hospital—accidents, illnesses, nonfunctioning body parts, etc. I had started thinking of the hospital as one of my workrooms at the North Pole—it was a place to mend broken dolls. I reasoned that Santa had to have a place just for this purpose. *Santa and his elves can make broken dolls as good as new, and so can the staff and doctors at the Children's Hospital. If civilization is to be judged by how it treats its little children, the hospital will be true proof that society has a soul.*

After I entered the hospital, I felt a spirit of reverence that followed us wherever we went throughout the evening. I had a wonderful nurse assigned to me who updated me on each patient before my visit. As I entered the rooms, all the little bodies, whether they had full casts on their bodies, bandages around their heads, or tubes in their mouths or noses, had one thing in common—a big smile. I wanted to be as close to them as possible. It's okay to take them by the hand; it's a lot better to take them by the heart.

If I could hug them, I did, but I was ever so careful of their hurt little bodies. I told each of them about Santa's love for every child. I wasn't in a hurry; I talked to them and I read to them. I took with me a beautifully illustrated copy of *The Night before Christmas*, which they enjoyed very much—especially when it was read to them by Santa himself. I definitely wanted them to open their presents while I was there.

Some of the conversations were full of gems. One little girl said, "Do you know what I want for Christmas, Santa?"

I answered, "What?" and was told, "I just want to go home."

She started crying, and so did I. I found out that children don't mind seeing Santa cry. Tears are often just the outward expression of love. One little boy said, "You won't forget where I'm at on Christmas Eve, will you Santa?"

I responded, "That's why I came to visit. I wanted to know exactly where you are."

Another little girl's smile changed to a grimace, and she said, "Santa, can you make my 'owie' go away?" I asked where it was, and she pointed down to her foot. I reached down and touched it and said, "Now, owie, you go away." Her smile came back.

After we had visited several children, the nurse told me that the child in the next room would be able to be home for Christmas. She had been in the hospital for approximately eight months with bad burns and had about the same number of operations in that amount of time. Her mother was sitting in a chair next to her when I went in and was reading the Bible to her. The girl was only six years old. I've always found that children can understand the stories in the Bible; they aren't difficult and are always told in story form. Of all the children's books available, I always considered the Bible to be the best.

The little girl looked up as I walked in and for a minute just stared at me. It was as though she couldn't believe I was really there. She whispered, almost under her breath, "Santa!" she said it ever so softly and in such a way that a love affair began immediately. There was so much love and belief in this one word and such a calm acceptance of the fact of Santa's reality that I was totally overcome. Those awful burns would never be a detriment to this girl's lovely spirit. Her mother moved out of the chair, and I moved in. Everything seemed to happen automatically, as though it had been rehearsed. I gave the child my best Santa hug; I was as tender as I could be, her hug was much less inhibited. I said, "I see you were reading the Bible."

She explained that they were reading the story of the baby Jesus. She looked at me and said, "Do you know the story, Santa?" She ask the question in a way that indicated that she wondered if Santa was a believer. I assured her that it was my very favorite of all the stories in the world.

She said, "Mine too." I looked at the mother and gave her an approving nod, and tears fell onto her cheeks.

I said, "I heard some very happy news. They told me you would get to go home for Christmas."

I expected a great showing of happiness, but she seemed a little sad. I needed to understand this reaction, so I said, "I've got to go out to my bag. I forgot your present."

I walked out but motioned for the mother to follow. I told the girl's mother of my concern and was told that her daughter was afraid to leave the hospital because the doctors and nurses had taken care of her every need for the last eight months. She said, "When there's a lot of pain, they can take it away. They've fed her and cleaned and clothed her. She's been here so long that it's kind of a home to her."

I told the mother that I would see what I could do to help with the transition, and we went back in.

I said, "So, tell me your name."

She said, "My name is Mary."

"No wonder you like the story of Jesus. His mother was named Mary."

She gave a little laugh. I handed her the present, and she set it on her bed. I asked her if she was going to open it, and she looked at her mother and got an approving nod. Inside the box she found a beautifully made stocking monkey. Her reaction suggested that I had just given her the very choicest of all dolls. She took it by the arms, stretched them out, wrapped them around her neck, and gave it a big hug.

I mentioned that this monkey needed a name. We played the name game for a while, and she settled on "Punkey." I said, "Punkey the monkey. That sounds good to me." The nurse, the mother, and I all gave our approval.

I asked her what else she wanted for Christmas. She had thought this through thoroughly. Every time she named an item, I wrote it down. She then waited until I finished before she went on. When we had assembled a reasonable list, I said, "Mary, I'm going to come over to your house on Christmas Eve, and I'll be there before you go to bed. As soon as you get home, you start getting everything ready for my visit. I really like chocolate chip cookies and milk. Will you make me some?"

She perked up and said to her mother, "Mom, as soon as I get home in the morning, will you help me make the cookies?"

All problems of going home had been instantly dismissed. Her mother looked at me and gave me a big smile. As I left, I said, "Now be sure to have the cookies ready. I'll see you in three days. Merry Christmas."

I didn't get home until 9:30PM; it took me that long to visit every child. I got many, many more hugs in the hospital that night. I could never get enough hugs. The thoughts came to me, *Hugs say a lot more than I can ever say. After all, you kind of talk to a person through a hug, you can say, 'Let's be friends,' 'I love you,' or even 'I feel so sorry for you.' However, words sometimes are just insufficient. Sometimes only a hug will do. Santa has to be a good hugger.*

When I finally arrived home, I gave Sarah a bigger and longer hug than usual. She said, "You're getting to be an expert hugger."

I laughed to myself and said, *I'm getting a lot of practice.*

She replied, "Your hugs could still use a little more work," and I gave her another

I had to work on Sarah's gift for Christmas. I was a little skeptical of my ability but wanted to give it a go. I worked on the project for two hours and finally went to bed a little later than usual.

14

Santa's Letters

I had only two more days left at the mall, and I was truly sorry to see my time there as Santa coming to an end. As I mentioned before, I always work hard right up until the end, so I made a check to see if there was anything left unfinished. Haley walked into the workshop and said, "I don't want it to end; I could make being an elf a lifetime occupation." I assured her from the bottom of my heart that with her warm personality, she would always be an elf. Being an elf and a Santa had taken on new meaning for both of us. I said, "Speaking of being an elf, will you please take this list and go over to the toy store and pick up each of these toys." I gave her the list I had made for Mary. I added, "Tell Mr. Henley that we appreciate his help with the last gift, but this is something Santa has to do." I gave her what I thought would be enough money to more than cover the purchase.

Haley came back about an hour later with many Christmas packages. She put them in Santa's workshop and went back for more. When she came back, it seemed like there were a lot more presents than I had ordered. She said, "Here's your change." She handed me about half the money I had given her. She said, "Mr. Henley let you pay for every present but gave you the Santa Claus discount, he said, 'After all, Santa made the toys in the first place."' Haley helped me take the packages to the car, and they filled it to the brim.

I found myself sitting on my throne and thinking, *Two more mall days and three more parties. Where did the time go?*

I must have been a little over melancholy. A little boy came up to me and said, "Santa, why are you so sad?"

I thought the truth would be the best answer, so I merely told him that in three more days, Christmas would be over and I wouldn't have anything to do for a whole year. He reminded me that I had lots of toys to make for next year. I'd almost forgotten about that.

Haley worked her way through the children and asked me if she could run down the hall to the music store for a minute. Assuming she needed a piece of music or some other item, I said, "I have it under control; take what time you need."

She came back in about a half hour and had a shopping bag from the store. Curiosity got the best of me, so I asked her what she had bought. She pulled the item from the bag and took it carefully from a nice case. She showed me an instrument made out of wood and said it is a tenor recorder. I pried a little more and asked what she planned to do with it. She told me that it wasn't for her but that she was going to give it to a little girl. She then revealed the whole story to me.

As she was playing her flute one day, a little girl diligently sat and watched her every movement. The girl was so enthralled with the music that she stayed right there until the flute came out the second time. The girl made sure she had a front-row seat for the next carol. Haley said that she went up to the little girl and said, "Thank you for sitting so quietly and listening to me play."

The girl told her, "I wish I could make such beautiful music!"

Haley said, "My heart just went soft. I asked the girl's mother for their names and address and played another song for them."

She told me the little girl's name was Macy and that the recorder was for her. She then showed me a letter she had written to Macy and a music book she had also purchased for her. The letter read as follows:

Dear Macy,

Here is a professional tenor recorder for you; it is just like a flute. This is what I started to play when I was about your age. I have also given you a music book that will teach you how to play the recorder. I want you to read the book with your mother and learn the first song in the book. I will come by your house in one month to hear you play and then will give you some lessons. I will need someone to take over my job as an elf someday, and by then, you will probably be playing the flute even better than I do.

Merry Christmas,

Haley the Elf

I told Haley how proud I was of her and how well she had done. She said, "I learned from the master giver."

One of the parties that night was for the company where the boss always played Santa Claus. Many days previously, I found myself driving around with a few minutes to spare, so I decided to stop at the company and try to talk to the boss. Evidently the employee whom I had left a card with on my previous visit had passed it on to the owner. When I stopped by, the owner was ready to see me.

He was kind of a timid, soft-spoken sort. We went into his office, and he closed the door behind us. He called his receptionist on the intercom and told her we were not to be disturbed. He then confided in me that he had been the Santa at the company party for the last twelve years and had never really liked playing the role. The only reason he continued year after year was that he thought the employees kind of expected it of him. I leaned closer to him and said, "Just between us two Santa's, it's a hard role to play." He sat back and relaxed a little; he had someone who understood his plight.

After I told him that he had been missing half the party every year waiting in the back in his Santa suit and that he would be better served this year by being among his employees while I played the role of company Santa, a sense of relief hit him. And then he started giving me party information. All he needed was a good reason to make the change. I told him not to tell anyone that he was not going to play Santa. I said, "I'm going to act as if I'm you and have some fun doing it." He thought it would be fun and gave me all sorts of information about what he did each year. I explained that I intended to duplicate what he did but with a lot of exaggeration. He agreed it would be fun.

At the party, when I sauntered out and in a timid voice said, "Ho, ho, ho. Merry Christmas," it about brought the house down. In the end, it turned out that my impression of him seemed to hit everyone's funny bone and endeared the owner to everyone who was there. At times, he laughed harder than anyone else.

I left a little earlier than usual the next morning to run a few errands. At one point, I stopped off at the Post Office to pick up my mail. One of the postal workers ran out and stopped me. She said, "I hope you don't mind. I put a few Santa letters in your box. I thought they were the type that needed special attention."

All kinds of questions popped into my mind, I said, "Do you get many letters to Santa?" She gave a little snicker and told me that the Post Office gets thousands of them. I wondered how they separated these particular letters out to give me. I said, "Does someone read all those letters?"

She answered, "Yes, I do. It's one of the things I enjoy at Christmas time. Oh, I confess that I just skim through many of them, but every once in a while there's one I have to stop and read carefully. It's better than reading a boring novel."

I was absolutely amazed. *If only I had her back at the North Pole*, I said to myself. *I've found another elf.*

I told her that she could put as many letters in my box as she wanted and encouraged her to do it. I loved her for what she was doing. I asked her for her name and was told, "Sue Spencer. It's really Susan, but I like to just be called Sue."

I got in the car and thought I'd better read a couple of the letters just to get the nature of what she thought was important. Each letter had its own special need, but the third one struck my heartstrings immediately. Its writer said, *Dear Santa, You don't need to bring me anything this year but could you help my mom. She has sore teeth and they hurt her a lot. Thank you, Chloe Palmer.*

All kinds of pictures went through my mind, and I spoke out loud and said, "A plea like this cannot be ignored."

I set all the letters on the opposite seat to read them later and headed for the mall. Again I spoke out loud and said, "I might be a little late getting to the mall, but because I have only one day to find help for this little girl, I have to make a stop."

Across the street from the mall was a dental clinic. I had read in the paper a while back that several of the dentists had taken a humanitarian trip to Guatemala to help with impoverished children who desperately needed dental work. I pulled into the parking lot, grabbed the letter, and walked into the clinic. I was in full Santa apparel as I walked right up to the receptionist counter. I asked if I might, as Santa Claus, visit with one of the dentists. I was invited to go right in. *The suit works every time*, I said to myself.

I sat down with a Dr. Bruce Richards. He asked how he could help me. I said, "I need a tooth fairy." And then I handed him the little girl's letter.

He read the letter, looked up at me, and said, "I can help you. What do you want me to do?"

I suggested that his secretary make a copy of the letter. It had the address and phone number on it, and I felt that I needed the original. When this task was completed, I told Dr. Richards I would see that this family received the proper notification of the services in the way of a gift from the little girl to her mother. I asked if his office could call them a few days after Christmas to make an appointment for her to come in. He informed me that they would handle all the necessary details and that she would be taken care of as though she were one of their finest clients. "Her teeth will not only stop hurting but also will look very beautiful."

I said in response, "My, that all happened kind of fast and was just a little too businesslike, but then I didn't have much time left. I want you to know that I admire what you're doing. I thank you for the skills you have acquired to make people's lives a little easier, and I also thank you for your generosity in helping."

He assured me that he was probably being blessed much more than those he helped; it was a wonderful feeling to be able to help others. He told me he had a very good reason for what he did. He said, "I was reading of someone in need one day and I thought to myself, 'I wonder why somebody didn't do something for them.' And then I realized that I am 'somebody.'" I gave him one of my cards and asked if he would let me know how it all turns out. A perfect new elf.

I walked out to the car thinking, *This is a wonderful world. I'm very privileged as a Santa to see the kinder side of life. The usual words of 'Christmas,' 'joy,' 'merry,' and 'happy' have all taken on a new meaning. Merriment and laughter are certainly present, but they're enhanced with large doses of love. I do think the giver gets a larger portion of blessings than the getter.*

I soon arrived at the mall. Haley was already there and had things underway. She was sitting in the big chair looking ever so elfish. She had a tiny baby on her lap, and the mother was busy taking a picture. I pulled out my little Nikon and took one myself. Oh, yes, I had decided much earlier in the year to always carry my own camera. Once in a while I arranged for a child or a brother and sister to sit in my chair while I snapped a picture. They loved it when Santa wanted *their* picture. I created a file in my computer entitled *What Santa sees*, and I routinely down-loaded the pictures for future viewing. It's true that a picture is worth a thousand words. Indeed, there was a beautiful story behind each shot.

The trophy shop made a delivery to me, and there were all my plaques. The token of appreciation was absolutely wonderful; it captured the meaning of the award perfectly. Yes, it ended up costing me more than I had estimated in my mind, but then it also was much better than I had imagined. With the scores around its edges, the coin looked real. The Santa and the reindeer looked as though they had been engraved by a master engraver, and my elf plaques were better than I had expected.

I gave the delivery person two more names, Sue Spencer and Dr. Bruce Richards, and asked if the trophy shop could possibly make up two more elf plaques in time for Christmas Eve. He said that everything was set up and ready and that two more plaques would be a simple process. I asked if the dies or whatever they used could be stored for use next year and was told that they would be given to me to use however I wanted. Thankfully, I had enough foresight to have taken Sue Spencer's and Dr. Richard's pictures the minute I thought of them as elves, and I gave both pictures to the trophy fellow.

Both Haley and I seemed to cherish each moment of the next-to-last day at the mall. We seemed to linger over each child; I was hardly ever in my seat. I loved to pick up a child and hold her or him up to a limb on a tree and say, "Charlie, can you come out for a minute?" just before the squirrel popped out. I had all the sequences memorized, and the children loved it. I would tell the children to say "Hello" to Charlie. As they did so, I'd let the squirrel know he could go back inside and eat more nuts, and away he'd go into his hole in the tree. The children would almost forget what they were there for until I reminded them. The days were all too short, and I began thinking, *What will I do when I won't be able to hear Haley play every day?* Along with scores of mall visitors, I had become a totally dedicated fan of her personality and music.

One day a very nice-looking, respectable young man approached Haley and asked her if elves ever went on dates. True to form, she said, "They surely do. I get off at six, and then I have to change my clothes. I hope we're not going anyplace fancy because I have only my Levi's."

He laughingly said, "You can wear your elf outfit if you want. You look great. I'll see you at six."

He walked off down the mall, and I said, "That was kind of fast wasn't it?"

She said, "He's passed by many times, and he always smiles at me. I confess that I've always smiled back, and I was hoping he would stop sometime." And then she added, "That's exactly what I wanted for Christmas." She and I had both forgotten to get his name.

The young man showed up right at six o'clock. We found out that his name was Matt West. Haley gave me a hug; I told her to have a good time and they were off.

I grabbed the box full of plaques and headed to the car. I got in and adjusted the radio to my favorite Christmas music station and headed for my nightly parties. These two parties would be my forty-sixth and forty-seventh for the season, and I had only one more tomorrow night. The parties had gone very well, and I was getting to be quite the Santa. I had certainly accumulated great volumes of Santa and Christmas materials from holding so many of them.

Something always happens that makes each party unique. At the last party of the night, as I was handing out a couple of awards I had been asked to present, a fellow came up and asked if he could take the microphone for a minute. He seemed to be doing this almost against his own will but had gotten up enough confidence to continue. He said to me, "I want to sing them a song."

I asked those gathered around nearby, "Is he this way at work?" and they all replied, "Yes," and then they laughed knowing he was just the opposite. We had been using a talented piano player as we were singing a medley of Christmas songs. The prospective singer said to the pianist, "Can you play 'I'll Be Home for Christmas'?" The positive nod was reassuring. I asked the group if they wanted to hear him sing and got a mixed reply. I asked if he was a good singer and was told that they had never heard him sing. His shy personality was one that was hard to refuse. With my encouragement, they all started clapping. I could tell that many of them thought they would have a good time laughing at him at work the next day.

He got up on the platform and nodded to the piano player who gave him a great intro after which he started to sing. This was probably the first time he had ever sung in public, but each note reflected his assurance that it was his favorite thing to do. It wasn't long until we all realized we were hearing something special. His rendition definitely made us want to be home for Christmas. He finished, handed me the microphone, and stepped down. There wasn't a dry eye in the group; he even got a standing ovation. He'll probably be requested from now on to sing at every party. He was humble, not knowing exactly how good he really was, and merely went back and sat down.

15

One More Day, One More Party

Soon after the party ended, I got in the car, started it, and began listening to Christmas music. Out loud I said, "One more day; one more party!"

When I got home, Sarah was waiting as usual but wasn't in a hurry to get to bed. She told me she just needed a little holding time. We like to sit with all the lights off, except the Christmas-tree lights, and turn on the fire in the hearth. There's something magical about those moments. A thousand thoughts that are never spoken and never have to be spoken go through our minds. Why ruin a moment of true love with words?

As we got underway the next day at the mall, I was thinking that this last day at the mall would probably be the busiest with last-minute shopping and all. Haley reported on her date, "We went and saw the movie *Elf*, and we already have a Christmas-night date planned."

I guess Haley and I had become so proficient that things just ran very smoothly. A lot of people by this time have all their shopping completed, but many like to come and walk the halls for no other reason than to participate in the Christmas spirit. I loved to watch them; everyone was beautiful.

We actually talked to a lot of adults and passed out advice freely. One mother looked a little distraught, and I asked if I could help her. She said, "My daughter wants a Christmas present I don't want her to have." I told her that kids don't always want what's best for them and asked her how old her daughter was. She told me she was sixteen. When I asked her what her daughter wanted for Christmas, she said, "A tattoo—just a simple little butterfly on her ankle." I've never known parents who want their children to deform the beautiful bodies the parents have nourished all their lives. She said, "What's a mother to do?"

I told her to tell her daughter to sit down and write a list of ten reasons why she shouldn't get a tattoo and then ten reasons why she should. "Only under those circumstances will you even consider letting her get one." My reasoning suggests that most people don't consider all the implications from making a decision, and once they do, they usually talk themselves out of taking a wrong direction.

One young man about sixteen years of age came by with his girlfriend and said, "Remember us?" It took me a while, but with a little coaxing, I remembered her as the girl who wanted a boyfriend for Christmas. They were still together! The girl stated, "You have really made me a believer, Santa."

At about two o'clock, Mr. Burgess—Haley's father—and several other mall officials paid us a visit. They handed Haley and me each an envelope that I assumed was our paycheck, and we both thanked them. Mr. Burgess said, "There's a little extra in there for both of you. This has been the best year the mall has ever had, and we think we owe it all to Santa and his elf."

After they left, I turned to Haley and said, "Will you please play 'Silent Night' one more time for Santa." She set about getting Freddy ready. "I'm surely going to miss listening to Freddy," I mused.

I gathered up a group of children and placed them in a circle around the toadstool. I asked how many of them knew "Silent Night," and the response was almost unanimous. Haley started playing, and they joined in singing. They sang with a reverence, about fifty small voices who knew how to treat a song. I listened and wept.

Perhaps for the last time, Haley and I hugged, knowing we would never forget this time together. We then closed down shop for the season.

Shortly afterward, I moved on to the last party of the year— or at least the last party of my first year as Santa. Would there be more years to come? This last party was full of joy. I handed out bonuses again, this time with names on the envelopes, and the boss gave a beautiful Christmas reading that he's been requested to give each year. It was a story about some children singing a song in a school Christmas program called "Christmas Love." Each letter of Christmas was held up by a child when its message was given. When the seventh child's turn came, by mistake she held the sign upside down, making it a *W* rather than an *M*. Instead of reading "CHRISTMAS LOVE," it read "CHRIST WAS LOVE." It was a beautiful story.

I kind of played the role of the MC at my last party because they had several talent presentations. It seemed that most of the talent came from within the company, and I thought it rather good. I was handed a list of the performers and the numbers they were doing. I merely added a little appropriate Christmas spirit between each number to keep the spirits high. I had prepared well.

I discovered that one of the performers had a son who was reaching the age to start driving, and I singled him out and said, "You'll need a lot of wisdom. There was a man like you who had a son who early in the year came to his father and said, 'Father, if I get good grades this year, can I have a new car for next Christmas?' His father said, 'Yes, if you'll also read the scriptures daily and get a haircut.' His son went away to school, and his grades improved dramatically. He came home, but his hair was still long. He told his father that he had been reading the scriptures daily and found that all the men in the Bible, Moses, John the Baptist, Samson, and even Jesus, had long hair, so maybe the haircut was asking too much." Then I spoke to the father and said, "This is where the wisdom comes in. The boy's father responded by saying, 'But did you also notice that Moses, John the Baptist, Samson, and Jesus *walked* wherever they went?'"

After a lady had sung a great variety of happy Christmas songs, I told about her going to the store to pick up a turkey for Christmas dinner. She had to have a very large one and couldn't find the proper size. She went to an assistant at the store and asked, "Excuse me. Do these turkeys get any bigger?" He told her, "No ma'am. They're all dead."

As usual, I told them to *make* a merry Christmas. "It's proper to *make* it meaningful so you can let those you are with know you love them. It's a time of year when they will allow you to do this."

I got home a little early and was thankful for the time. I had a big day coming up on Monday, the day before Christmas, and I needed to make a list so I wouldn't forget anything:

1. Deliver elf plaques; pick up last two plaques.

2. 5:00PM Deliver token of appreciation

3. Meet with Mabel and Ann

4. Deliver sore-tooth present.

5. Presents for Mary

6. Haley's present

Because the next day was Sunday, I had a day off. We went to church, came home, and had our usual Sunday roast and mashed potatoes. And we then rested the rest of the afternoon. We headed back over to the church that evening to an annual Christmas program performed by a Polynesian family in our church and some of their friends. Their smooth tones and pure faith always made this program the highlight of the season and a congregational tradition. It was nice to sit back and let someone else do the entertaining.

I hit the ground running the next morning. While eating my breakfast instead of reading the newspaper, I started reading some more of the Post Office letters from the children. After reading about eight of them, I stopped. I said to Sarah, "There is so much more we could have done if only we had more time and, yes, funds." I set the letters aside and thought to myself, *I'll see what I can do later*. At that point, I put one of the letters in my pocket.

I started my day with a visit to the home of the mother with sore teeth. I had Sarah wrap a small box with a note in it that said,

> *Dear Mommy. I hope this gift will help you smile. Please call Dr. Bruce Richards' office. You'll find his phone number and address in the phone book. He'll be happy to do whatever is necessary to help you with your teeth. His office will also be calling you for an appointment.*

The note was signed, *Suzy*.

I drove up to the house, went up the front sidewalk, and knocked on the door. I guessed that it was Suzy who opened the door. I asked if her name was Suzy, and she said it was. I told her that I had received the letter she wrote to Santa and that I had brought a gift for her to give her mother on Christmas morning. "You should let her know that the gift is from you. This will help her get her teeth to stop hurting. Run in right now and put this under the Christmas tree." I then gave her a present of her own.

She took the present, said "Thank you, Santa," closed the door, and was gone. I heard her mother call, "Who was it, Honey?" Suzy answered, "Just Santa Claus."

I went from there to the mall to pick up the rest of the plaques. As I walked through the mall, I was able to pick up a few hugs from some of the children. My first stop was at the toy store, where Mr. Henley dropped what he was doing and came right over to me. The first words out of his mouth were, "I know you're very busy today, so just tell me what you want and I'll round it up for you." He was ready to help with another toy order. I told him that I was there for a different reason. I said, "Mr. Henley, once in a while people should be rewarded for what they do. Your ability to capture the spirit of Christmas has gained you that distinction, so I would like to make you an Honorary Santa's Elf." And then I handed him the plaque.

His was a spirit of giving rather than receiving, and he didn't quite know how to react. He said, "Oh my, this is an honor I never expected to receive." He kind of stroked the plaque and said, "I have a perfect place for this," and he pointed to a wall just over the cash register. He stated that it would always be there to let people know he cared more about children than business. I couldn't have been happier that a plaque could make such a statement.

I left the mall, drove across the street to the dental clinic, and met again with Dr. Richards. I told of my meeting with Suzy that morning and of how I had made the delivery. He stated that there would be one surprised mom on Christmas morning and added, "Isn't it fun?" I told him I would like to make him an Honorary Santa's Elf and handed him the plaque. His reaction was enough to know that he was moved, and he told me that I could count on him at any time.

I wasn't able to get the address of our NBA point guard, so I headed for the arena where the team's offices were located. As

usual, I met with the receptionist and told her my mission. I was
told to wait a minute and then was introduced into the general
manager's office. I had seen this man many times on the news
and a couple of times at games, but meeting him face to face was
an honor. He was on my nice list.

I told him of the incident with his point guard and of how
happy it had made a couple of fans. I handed him the plaque
and asked if he would deliver it. He looked at the plaque and,
as any good general manager would do, considered the mileage
he might get out of it. It seems as though the NBA-associated
personnel are always eager to promote public relations with
their players and equally eager to make the public aware of all
they do. He asked if I would like to make a presentation at the
next game, which would be the day after Christmas. I thought
of the implications. The father and son would be at the game,
and the presentation might make them appear as a charity case.
Besides, the player had always shunned publicity. I asked if it
could just be given to him quietly. He agreed with my reasoning
and said he would present it himself.

From there, I went to the Post Office, knocked on the
back door, and was invited in. Several of the workers stopped
what they were doing, and Sue Spencer was called in from the
front. I said, "Sue, anyone who loves children as much as you
do deserves to be one of Santa's elves." And then I handed her
the plaque. She was stunned. Some of her fellow workers came
up with cameras, and we had a session of picture taking. Sue
told me she had placed some more letters in my box. One of the
workers volunteered to run and get my mail for me, and I was
soon on my way to the next stop.

When I went into the Post Office several weeks later, her
plaque was hanging in a very visible place on the wall. There
was a greatly enlarged picture of me granting her elf status. In

visiting the Post Office subsequently, I was never recognized without my suit.

I made an unscheduled stop at Pets Are Us. I pulled out the letter I had stuck in my pocket earlier and reviewed it again. It read, *Dear Santa. I hope you can help me. Do you give pets for Christmas? My dog Buddy died, and I miss him so much. I have already bought him a Christmas present. If I don't get a dog, I'll know you don't give live things for Christmas. I hope you do. Tommy. P.S. Buddy was a beagle dog.*

The pet shop did not have a beagle at the time, but they had just posted a notice from a family who had five beagle puppies for sale. I wrote down the phone number and gave the family a call. When someone answered the phone, I said, "Hi, this is Santa. Do you still have any beagle puppies available?"

They had two left. I asked them where they were located and was given their address. They were about fifteen miles out of town. I had no time to drive all the way out, pick up the puppy, and make the delivery, so I said, "May I read you a letter."

I read them Tommy's letter and told them that because of my Santa commitments, I didn't have the time to make the trip. The lady on the phone said, "If you have the address, we'll deliver the puppy for you." I couldn't believe my good luck, but I knew that luck didn't have anything to do with it. I had to work out how to pay them.

After putting me on hold for a couple of minutes, the lady came back and said, "Is it okay if we just make this our Christmas special gift?" I was prepared to pay quite a large sum, knowing that dogs are costly. She told me they would leave right now and would have him delivered in less than an hour. She also promised to tell Tommy that Santa had read his letter and that he had made the arrangements for his new Buddy. It was way too late for an elf plaque to be made, but I would see they received one even if it was late for Christmas.

When I arrived at Barbara Barwick's home, she was busy wrapping presents. She had several nieces and nephews with her and was helping them wrap their family presents. They were very surprised to open the door and see me. Barbara turned around at all the commotion and almost slipped by calling my non-Santa name. She caught herself and said, "Santa, come in. We were about to have a sandwich, and you can join us."

I grabbed one of her little nieces, put her on my lap, and sat at the table. Everyone gathered around and I said, "Did you all know that your Aunt Barb is secretly one of my very special elves?"

They looked at her in amazement. She in turn looked at me in amazement. I pulled out the plaque with her picture on it and said, "See, there she is, and this says she is one of my elves."

They passed it among themselves and were awestruck at their aunt's secret. Barb finally got to see the plaque. I guess the moment was precisely the right one because she got all emotional. I handed her a paper towel and then said, "Well, where is my sandwich?"

We ate together and laughed. I told a little story about Rudolph and about how one of the elves had given him the wrong hay. "As a result, his nose wouldn't shine." I told them all to go to bed early that night. I gave Barb a big hug and told her thanks once again.

From there, I went to Alex's home. His wife and children were getting ready to take a box of groceries to a needy neighbor. I wondered how many little acts of kindness happen on Christmas Eve. I thanked Alex for his beautiful pictures and talked to each of his children separately. I gave Alex his plaque and told his family that he had now become an elf. He said "We'll hang it right next to our picture," as he pointed to the wall where a picture of him, his wife, and me was proudly displayed. Of course, we then had a picture session with each of his kids.

I had purposely set enough time aside to visit Haley. I had told her mother that I would arrive about three o'clock and asked if she could make some kind of excuse to have Haley at home then. When I arrived, I heard beautiful flute music coming from the house. I wished the whole world could have heard it. It was a difficult arrangement of "Deck the Halls with Boughs of Holly." Every note was calculated to present the joy of the message. The fah lah lahs were a hundred trills, and the end of "'Tis the season to be jolly" sounded as though the notes were laughing. I waited out in the cold to hear the finish and then rang the doorbell. The door opened almost immediately. Haley's never slow at anything she does. She let out a loud scream, said "Santa!" and flew the door wide open. She called to her mother, "Look who's here!" She then said, "I already miss it. Do you?" I assured her I did. We sat down and talked over some of our experiences, and both of us agreed that we loved every minute of it.

I said, "Haley, I picked you up a little gift." I handed her a small, wrapped box, and she asked if she had to wait until Christmas to open it. Her mother and I both agreed that she didn't have to wait. She tore off the wrapping and opened a jewelry box. Inside, she found a gold locket. On the front, I had engraved a beautiful scrolled elf. She opened it. On the inside, I had placed a picture of Haley as an elf on one side, and the other side had the picture of her holding the little baby on the big throne. To say that Haley was quite emotional is an understatement. She started sobbing openly and said, "It's so beautiful! It's so beautiful! I never want to forget the best Christmas season I have ever had, and this will help me to remember it always." She told me she had a present for me. "However, it isn't quite complete." She wondered if she could come over later tonight to deliver it. I couldn't think of anything I'd rather be doing.

When I returned to the car, I tried to put into words my feelings: It may sound by now as if everyone involved is exaggerating the events of this season. All I can say, however, is that after my elves and I experienced one wondrous moment after another, we truly lived the spirit of Christmas. Everything was then more meaningful; each kind act was magnified; and love was a common denominator in all that happened. I would rather err on the side of exaggeration than be guilty of not giving enough merit where it's due.

My final stop before going home was a visit to Mr. Harrington's home. As I pulled up, I noticed the TV van had already arrived. It looked like the newspaper people were there also. They had awaited my arrival, and they joined me as we walked up to the front door. They couldn't stop raving about how great my suit looked.

As expected, Mr. Harrington opened the door himself and was a little startled upon seeing the camera crews. Regaining himself, he invited us into the front hall and asked the camera crew and the writers would mind waiting while he surprised his grandchildren with Santa's visit. He thought it would be nice if the camera man could just stick the camera in and record Santa's visit. The house was adorned with the presence of Christmas everywhere. Evidently, Mrs. Harrington liked to collect Santa Claus dolls because they were displayed on the stairs and in the windowsills and on a table and in almost every other place. He opened the door to a large family room, and it was full of family members. In my bag, I had the leftover candy canes from the mall. I distributed them as I went around wishing everyone a Merry Christmas.

After getting everyone's attention, we invited the media people in. And then I said, "Santa is here for a very special reason. Your grandpa, father, and husband has been chosen out of all the people in the whole city to receive a very special award.

Santa chooses one person each year to let that person know how much he or she is appreciated by the whole community. This year I have chosen Mr. James T. Harrington and would like to present to him this Token of Appreciation,"

I then handed the gold token to Mr. Harrington, as he looked at it and read the inscriptions and turned it over, it was easy to see he was moved. Everyone started clapping, and the occasion was truly a proud moment for him. I then handed him the whole plaque and showed him how the coin fit. To himself, he read the attached letter. His wife had moved to stand by his side, and she handed him a hanky. He then read the letter out loud to all and turned to me and said, "Thank you, Santa."

Mr. Harrington found a moment while pictures were being taken and questions asked to let me know that this award would find a way among his cherished possessions. I told him he had found a way into the hearts of all in the community and thanked him. He was pensive for a moment and then turned to me and asked, "Is there any way to get in touch with you in the future?" I handed him my card. He looked at it and laughed a little and said, "Just what I would have expected." He put the card in his pocket. I told myself that I definitely needed to watch the Channel 4 news tonight and read the paper in the morning.

I had one more stop to make. I had to deliver a car full of presents to Mary as promised. I parked in the driveway and hurried to the front door. The door opened before I even rang the bell; it was Mary in all her glory. She was dressed beautifully and was walking great with her one crutch. I yelled "Merry Christmas" out loud, and it was time for hugs. Her mother and father asked me in, but I told them I needed some help getting all the packages in. It took all three of us loaded to the hilt to manage the packages. We spread them around the tree, and it almost filled their little room. I pulled out the long list we had made in the hospital together and checked it over against the number of packages, all the while making quite a point that everything was there.

I finally said, "There, that will do it. I don't think we missed a thing. Mary, I want you to know that you are the very first child in the whole world to get their presents this Christmas Eve."

One present less would not have accomplished the purpose of this Santa visit. Mary was wandering around the room in total amazement and then turned to me and said, "Here are your cookies and milk." In my entire life, I had never tasted a cookie so good and never expect to again. The cookies were so good that I asked for another. I said, "You just can't eat a chocolate-chip cookie without a glass of cold milk. It's like the old question of which came first, the chicken or the egg? Did the milk make the cookies taste better, or did the cookies make the milk taste better?"

I told Mary that she would have to wait to open all her presents until in the morning, and she seemed thrilled to comply. Then, one of those special moments came again. She turned away from all the packages and seemingly put the glitter of Christmas behind. She walked over to me with an awareness far beyond her age and said, "This is the night Jesus was born." I took her in my arms and said, "And his mother was named Mary." To myself, I said, *Mary will never forget this Christmas Eve as long as she lives. This was important to me; my job is to make good memories.*

I arrived home at about 6:30PM just as Ann and Mabel arrived. Previously, we had invited them over for a little Christmas dessert and a lot of Christmas spirit. They handed me a wrapped present and told me to put it under the tree for Christmas morning. Mabel gave me a wink. They were both alone but had places to go later in the evening and family dinners tomorrow. Mabel walked in and said, "Okay, Sarah, where's my plate of Christmas cookies?" This was Sarah's standard offering to those near us each Christmas, they both looked forward to it every year. Sure enough, the plates were ready but with more cookies than usual.

I said, "I have something for you two ladies." I had not yet changed out of my Santa suit. I said, "This is a gift from Santa."

I handed them their plaques and said, "I have thought of you as my elves all season long. You were my very first elves, and you have certainly earned the right to belong to this order."

After listening to their many reasons why I shouldn't have done it, "You have been so busy," "You have so many others to look after," "We didn't do all that much," and so forth, I got serious with them. I sat down opposite them and took one of their hands in each of mine and said, "Santa has found out that he cannot be effective without the aid of great elves. I love you both deeply for helping and wish I could give you much more. We are very blessed to have you as neighbors and friends and you are in every way true Santa Elves. You have helped make this a life-changing event for Sarah and me. Merry Christmas."

Ann broke the solemnity of the occasion by asking, "What are we going to do next year?"

They had to run to get to their other appointments, but they had no sooner left than the doorbell rang. Haley and her parents were there. They were on their way to another family party, but Haley's mother said, "Nothing would do but that you would have Haley's Christmas present on Christmas Eve."

Haley said, "I hope you will like it," as she handed me a small package.

I opened it ever so slowly. I thought I knew what it was and was hoping it was what I thought. Sure enough it was a CD made by Haley herself of all her Christmas music. On the CD was a picture of Haley in her elf outfit. She had entitled it, "Have Your Elf a Merry Little Christmas." She told me she was recording the last song, "Deck the Halls," just before I arrived at her house today. I thought, *Thank goodness I have that moment to replay over and over.*

It was the best gift I could ever receive, and I couldn't wait to play it. She showed us that she was wearing her locket. I got another hug and they were off. That night would be spent sitting in front of the tree with only its lights on, with Christmas cookies and Haley's flute playing in the background. It turned out to be my best Christmas Eve ever.

We turned on the television in time for the ten o'clock news. We listened to a great opening sequence with the anchor saying, "We want to show you a visit Santa made to a grandpa and his grandchildren." He went on to say that it was a special visit that night, and then showed the presentation of the *Token of Appreciation* to James Harrington. A closeup of the *Token* and a beautiful dialogue regarding a gift that would keep on giving for years to come—followed by a picture of Mr. Harrington wiping at a slight tear on his cheek—was enough to affirm that the effort had been worth it.

After the presentation had been made, I said, "Sarah, listen to this!" The TV news anchor asked if this would be an annual award given each year from now on, and I told him I hoped it would. "But somebody has to be very good to earn the award." He asked how the recipient is chosen, and I said, "It will never be based on who gives the *most* but on who gives the *best*." He closed with, "We'll check with you next year. Good luck tonight in making all your deliveries."

16

Christmas Morning

Sarah always rises much earlier on Christmas morning than on other mornings of the year, a carryover habit from childhood. She doesn't want to miss one minute of Christmas day. And then we always go straight to the tree to see if Santa has been here. It's a yearly contest to see who has sneaked in during the night to leave the last present under the tree. Typically, there are always a few more presents than expected.

On this occasion following my stint as Santa, Sarah insisted that I open the first present, which was a warm flannel robe. She then opened a pair of slippers I had seen her admiring in the store one day. We opened a couple of other stocking-filler presents, and then she handed me my last gift, which I opened carefully. It was a beautifully framed picture of me in my Santa suit, and it was sitting on top of a full Santa cape. The picture was a memory of my first year as Santa and would look wonderful hanging in my den. I told her I had a couple more presents for her and gave her a scrolled paper with a red ribbon tied around it. She carefully opened it and found a poem I had written to her. It read as follows:

Will You Be Mine Again?

You know I'm not a poet,
But I'll attempt to put in rhyme,
That after all our years together,
I'm so glad that you're still mine.

Of all the girls I knew back then,
You're the one I chose.
Why you accepted my proposal,
Heaven only knows.

But as I'm someone different now,
So I thought I'd ask again.
Because I'm not the same guy I was
When I asked you way back then.

You changed your name once for me
To Mrs. Robert Field.
Your name will have to change again
If once more to me you'll yield.

I'm asking this for myself,
But think it's a very good cause.
What I'm asking now, Sarah,
Is will you be Mrs. Santa Claus?

She looked at me and said, "You actually wrote a poem! I love it. And yes, I'll be your Mrs. Santa Claus."

She didn't know whether to laugh or cry and started walking out of the room. I asked her where she was going and was told she had to call Mable and Ann so she could read them the poem. I said, "Wait a minute. A ring always comes with a proposal." And then I handed her another gift.

She opened it and inside found a diamond-cluster pinky ring. Inside the band I had the jeweler engrave, "Mrs. Santa Claus." Now the tears did come, but I stopped her again and said, "You can't be Mrs. Santa Claus and not have a proper dress," and I handed her another gift. Inside was a red velvet dress made of the same material as my Santa suit. Instead of a fur collar, it had a white lace edge with the same lace around the wrist to match. There was a dust cap of red velvet edged again with the white lace and a sprig of holly on one side. The dress was ankle length, and with it was a beautiful, long, white Victorian apron.

My Sarah didn't respond with words; once again, a hug expressed her feelings much better.

We didn't have a lot of time to enjoy everything. Mable and Ann were coming over for our annual Christmas breakfast—Sarah's famous Swedish pancakes. When they arrived, it was show-and-tell time. Nothing would do but for Sarah to read the poem aloud to them and then show the engagement ring. They of course had sewn the dress for me but wanted to see it on Sarah. With a promise to try it on right after we ate, Sarah said, "But first we have to have breakfast."

Now here's one of life's puzzles I've never figured out. When something is as good as Sarah's Swedish pancakes, why does she serve them only once a year?

The rest of the day went as usual. We didn't have our children and families coming because both of our kids live out of town and it was also the in-laws turn to have them over for Christmas this year.

I scanned the morning paper to see what they had written of my visit to Mr. Harrington. The article was much like last evening's television presentation, but the writer had added my address: P.O. Box 1225. Sarah and I sat down together and watched *It's a Wonderful Life*, a Christmas tradition, and then we settled in for another Christmas tradition—the Christmas day football game. At some point during the game, Sarah said to me, "Life is good." In turn, I responded, "Life is *very* good."

17

Becoming Santa

I woke up the next morning with nothing to do. I thought to myself, *I'll just use the morning to wrap up all my Christmas business.*

I got my Santa suit ready to send to the cleaners and then decided to do a business accounting. I hadn't yet opened my pay envelope from the mall, and I also didn't know if I'd overspent on all the help we gave everyone.

After listing all the outgo, I came up with a figure of $2,835. Using my little book of donations, I added a couple I hadn't recorded as yet, and the total turned out to be $2,700. I was $135 short, but I was sure we could make that up without hurting ourselves.

I next opened my pay envelope from the mall. True to the agreement, there was a check for $7,000. I turned another check over, and it was written for $1,500 and designated as a bonus. I called Sarah in and said, "Look what the mall has given us for a bonus," and handed her the check. She wasn't even aware they had already paid me $7,000 for my regular salary and was stunned when I showed that check to her. She walked out of the room with the bonus check still in her hand, and I heard the cupboard door open and the jar come out.

I had received all party payments except for two companies and had $4,600 to deposit from that source. I made a deposit slip out for $11,600 and planned on a trip to the bank later. I dialed Mr. Burgess's number. After a short pause, he came on line. I thanked him for the bonus, and he said, "We all received larger bonuses this year, thanks to you." I was hoping that Haley also got a bonus and was told they had given her $500. Before we said goodbye, he said they definitely wanted me back next year. "We'll be pleased to arrange an even larger contract."

I had a large stack of mail on the desk, and I already knew that most of the items were letters to Santa. I sorted them out and found several from companies I had visited. The company letters brought back memories, but they all had about the same theme: *Best Christmas party ever.* In every instance, they hoped they could secure my services for next year. I made a note to myself to make a list of all the companies, including contact information, addresses, and phone numbers. And I reflected that I should write them all thank-you cards. *I have plenty of them already printed,* I said to myself.

I finally got to the Santa letters—almost 50 of them. I wondered if I would find more of them at the Post Office. The minute I started reading, I became Santa again. I was overwhelmingly drawn in by the needs of the writers. I reached for a notebook and started making notes on each letter I read. I assigned each letter a number and wrote it on the letter and then made my notes by a corresponding number in my notebook. I had already concluded earlier that all children's needs were always valid. I reasoned, *Children have no propensity to lie.* I had also determined that some needs should not have to wait to be taken care of. Christmas was 364 days away—way too long to wait to solve some of these needs. And then I thought, *What would Santa do?*

After about four more hours, I finished reading the letters. Sarah stepped in once to see what I was doing, went out without saying a word, and came back in with a sandwich and a glass of milk. She had silently interpreted that what I was doing was important. I would definitely have to give serious consideration to what *could* be done. The bottom line, of course, was that the people of this world are definitely in need of a Santa Claus—a real Santa. Their needs are compelling and demand assistance. Loads of issues popped into my mind. *Yes, most of the children associated with these letters could be helped some by simple means. But the needs of others could become quite involved. In fact, more will be needed to help them than one man's ability allows. And where would all the funds come from?*

While dwelling on those thoughts, I glanced at one of the letters. It was from a little boy who simply ended his request by saying, *Please help me.*

Out loud I said, "How can I do more." That statement turned into, "I must do more." I immediately came back to one of the earlier lessons I had learned: *Somebody should certainly help, and I am somebody.*

Time had flown, and there was probably just enough of the day left for me to get all my chores completed. I retrieved my Santa suit and bank deposit and told Sarah I wouldn't be gone very long. I drove to the cleaners and the bank and decided to stop of at the Post Office. However, I unexpectedly had second thoughts about the Post Office and decided to go there after hours from now on. I couldn't explain that rationale, but I still clearly had an inclination that told me to stay anonymous. I had previously decided to keep my Post Office box.

That night I settled in to watch my NBA basketball team play. It was kind of pleasing to know that a father and son and the rest of their family were sitting high up in one of the executive suites watching a professional ballgame in person for the first time. I had a difficult time concentrating on the game. Questions and issues associated with the letters kept going through my head, especially later when I went to bed and couldn't sleep.

As we were moving around the house the next morning, I said, "Sarah, could we just sit down and talk for a minute? I need your help."

Because she knows my every mood, she looked at me knowingly and asked, "Is this going to be a serious discussion?"

I responded, "It's serious enough that I need my best advisor's help with it."

We went in the office and sat next to each other in front of the desk. I picked up the stack of letters and placed them in front of her. I then said, "Sarah, I have to admit that I've never enjoyed anything in my life as much as I did being Santa this year, and I believe I was a good Santa."

She said, "I've been so proud of you the last two months. You truly came alive and did so much good for so many people."

I said, "That's just it; I've come to the realization that there's so much more I must do. I have the feeling that this year was just a practice year, that there is something bigger coming. I've found that I got better as I understood the Santa business. Early on, I realized that I improved with the passage of time. I knew almost from the beginning that I would be a much better Santa at the end." All of these letters tell me one thing, there is a need for a good Santa,

I told her I had to be very realistic; I just couldn't go up to the North Pole and make toys the rest of the year. I was emphatic that I didn't plan on opening a Santa Claus business or a nonprofit Santa foundation because that is just not the way Santa does things. "Santa was never a fundraiser—only a fund spender. I just like being able to do good for others and would be satisfied doing just that the rest of my life. If I weren't inhibited by accounting to others for each penny spent, decisions would not be based on the amount of the funds but on the extent of the need."

We then got into the financial part. In two months, our Social Security would start, as we both would be turning sixty-five years of age. I had paid heavily into Social Security over the years and expected a reasonable amount. Sarah had not paid into the program, but a wife is entitled to receive one-half of her husband's monthly Social Security check, so together our earnings would be a considerable figure. I reasoned, "We can buy food and pay the monthly bills on this amount alone. The retirement pay I lost was supposed to provide money for home improvements, a trip once in a while, and some of the niceties of life, but by being Santa, I've earned more than I expected. And if my Santa earnings were allocated over the year, they would provide us with about a thousand dollars extra a month. So I'm sure we could get by, barring any unexpected bills being dropped on us. And we have some decent savings that will help if needed."

Sarah stopped me and said, "Robert let's not go any further. We've always planned that you'll retire at age sixty-five, and I believe that's what you should do. What you do with your time has always been up to you. You may not be able to help as many people as you want, but isn't helping one better than helping none? And don't worry; we'll always somehow make do. Now let me add just one more thing. I know you, and I know that your goodness and ability will always find a way to accomplish what you want to do." And then she added, "I heard a quote once and we'll just have to live by it: 'Live simple so others can simply live.' I believe we can do that."

She then said she had to get the clothes out of the washer and to call her if I needed anything else. As she was leaving, she poked her head back in the door and said, "A Santa is needed, and you're the best there is."

I went to the pantry and pulled out the money jar. With the mall bonus check, there was $1,700 available. I thought, *Well, I can reimburse our $135.* And then I thought, *No, that will be our contribution for the New Year.* It wasn't a large amount, but it was more than I had originally started with.

I went to the bank and opened a special account for my Santa funds. I explained to the bank that some—or even most—of the checks I deposited would be made out to Santa. The bank arranged things through a series of signatures so that I could now deposit checks as Santa Claus. "Hooray," I said. "Santa has a bank account." A debit card was given to me in my name and would be the sole source of funds withdrawal. I knew that banks cannot give out customer information, so I knew I would be protected as to my identity.

This was going to be a major decision. The question was not, *Do I want to be Santa?* That was a given; I loved everything about being Santa Claus. The question was, *How do I become Santa?*

I had come to the conclusion long ago that I didn't want it to be merely a role I was playing; I wanted to be *real.* I knew there were solutions, and I knew I would just have to find them. Any project of this magnitude would have to be given proper consideration. Every time I thought it might be more than I could bite off, I returned to the letters and thought, *These are real problems that no one else seems to be solving. What would Santa do in this situation?* I knew he would figure out a way of taking out the "un" and just leave "happiness." The outcome was worth the time it deserved, and I now had plenty of that.

At about 6:30PM that evening, I decided to make my trip to the Post Office. I parked in front, and when I was satisfied no one would see me, I went in and picked up the mail. I couldn't believe how much there was. There were still quite a few children's letters; I noticed they were all postmarked just before Christmas. I also noticed one from James Harrington and thought, *Isn't it nice of him to send me a thank-you note?* That prompted me to return home to write all of the donors a letter telling them how their funds had been used and how they had brought joy to others.

I went home ready to go to work, but when I arrived, Mabel and Ann were there for their weekly game night. Once a week we got together to play games and have fun, but this tradition had been interrupted because of my Christmas work. We played four games of Rummikub, and I didn't win any of them. The ladies in my life took their games seriously. The night, however, did take my mind off business for a while, which I really needed.

The next morning, I wrote a detailed letter and sent it to each person who had donated money during the Christmas season, including the company that gave me a $1,000 bonus. I recounted for them each appropriate story associated with their donations and let them know of all the people they had helped and how much their help was appreciated.

I then sorted my mail. The two companies that hadn't paid as yet sent checks and appreciations. I next opened a letter from a person I had never heard of. The letter read as follows:

Santa,

Please find a check enclosed in the amount of $2,000. James Harrington mentioned that these funds would be used for a very good cause.

James Arnott

Shelby Corporation

I was stunned. *Does this kind of thing happen often?* My decision-making had suddenly become much easier. I reached for the James Harrington letter, sliced open the envelope, pulled out the letter, and read:

Dear Santa,

> *I want to thank you once again for the beautiful plaque and token. Once in a while a person receives something that makes all his efforts worthwhile, and your offering filled that need.*

> *It seems we use the same dentist, Dr. Bruce Richards. When I told him of my coin of appreciation (by the way, I let everyone know about it, and I'm quite proud of it), he told me of his dealings with you and showed me his elf plaque. You see, I help fund, in a way, his humanitarian trips to Guatemala. I was thinking that I'm helping a lot of kids thousands of miles away but none right here in my own backyard.*

> *I pride myself on the fact that I am a good judge of character and was hoping you would have the time to help some of my hometown kids. To get you started, I have enclosed a check and will send more when needed. No need to write me with your decision; I have full faith in your judgment. Don't ever miss the opportunity of making anyone happy because of the lack of funds.*

> *Oh, by the way, I have mentioned this to several of my investment group colleagues, and*

they may also want to donate funds. Don't worry about keeping an accounting. It wouldn't be a proper gift if we were doing it just for a tax deduction.

Thank you again for helping an old man believe his life has been worth something.

Sincerely,

James Harrington

I opened the folded check and found the sum to be $20,000. I literally sat there and sobbed. *How could people be so kind?* I was so thankful that I had this moment alone. Sometimes a person just doesn't want to inhibit a good cry. *Now,* I thought, *my decision has been made.* After pulling myself together, which I wasn't in a hurry to do, I turned my thoughts to Sarah.

About that time, Sarah looked into the office. She took one look at me and could tell I had shed a few tears. She said, "Oh Robert, what's wrong?"

I told her, "It's not what's wrong; it's what's right."

She then said, "We're going to have another one of those talks, aren't we?"

I said, "You know how you are always saying something will work out and it always does? Well, it certainly has this time." I showed her the two letters and the two checks. She sat back in her chair to process the information she had been given.

I said to Sarah, "When something as unexpected as this happens that opens the door for you to follow your dreams in every way and when you realize you now have the go-ahead, you sometimes begin to doubt your capabilities. I have people placing a great deal of trust in me. Do I have the competence to accomplish the responsibilities it would take to effectively find and help those in need?"

She asked, "What is it that you're not qualified to do?"

I honestly couldn't answer her. She then asked, "You do love what you've been doing for the last two months, don't you?"

She told me she had never seen me so happy. "If making others happy is what brings you happiness, then you better do it. Santa of all people deserves and should be happy."

I turned to her and said, "There's only one more thing I have to know before I make the plunge. Will you be happy? I mean, we're in this together. If you're not satisfied with this lifestyle, if we're doing this just for me, then it's not worth it."

She assured me that she had received as much joy from this service as I did. She then said, "My work is to have things done here that will allow you to do your work out there. I could not wish for a better life, and besides I have already changed my name to 'Mrs. Santa Claus' and have a ring to prove it."

I said, "The more I know you, the more I understand you, and the more I understand you, the more I love you and appreciate all that you are. Let's get started."

She said, "I thought we already had."

She went back to the kitchen, and I headed for my office.

I started reading letters again and found myself sorting out all the needs and making plans as to how to take care of them. I asked myself, *How does Santa give gifts when it's not Christmastime?* The answer came easily: *He simply does it anonymously as Santa Claus.*

At that point, I knew why I wanted to remain anonymous.

After a couple of hours of planning and laying out my day for tomorrow, I thought, *Well, I guess I'm a full-time Santa now.*

*Maybe I don't have reindeer that can fly or a toy factory at the North Pole, or maybe I can't go all around the world in one night— but I **can** do everything else. My suit is real, my beard is real, and to those I help, I'm very real.*

And then it hit me and sent thrills through my body. *I **have** become Santa Claus. I **am** Santa Claus. For the rest of my life I **will be** Santa Claus. People everywhere can honestly tell their children there is a **real** Santa Claus.*

I said—almost too loudly—as I headed to bed, "Merry Christmas to all, and to all a good night!" I knew at that moment why Santa loved to say that.

The End

Richard Robbins